HISTORIC
AIRCRAFT

HISTORIC AIRCRAFT

STEVE McDONALD

SHOOTING STAR PRESS

A QUINTET BOOK

This edition published in 1995 for:
Shooting Star Press, Inc.
230 Fifth Avenue, Suite 1212
New York, NY 10001

ISBN 1-57335-294-2

This book was designed and produced by
Quintet Publishing Limited
6 Blundell Street
London N7 9BH

Creative Director: Terry Jeavons
Designer: Wayne Blades
Project Editor: Lindsay Porter
Editor: Peter Arnold
Picture Researcher: Steve McDonald

Typeset in Great Britain by
Central Southern Typesetters, Eastbourne
Manufactured in China by
Regent Publishing Services Limited
Printed in Singapore by
Star Standard Industries (Pte) Ltd

CONTENTS

INTRODUCTION — 6

HISTORIC AIRCRAFT COLLECTION — 10

MAJOR COLLECTIONS AND MUSEUMS — 94

INDEX — 95

ACKNOWLEDGEMENTS — 96

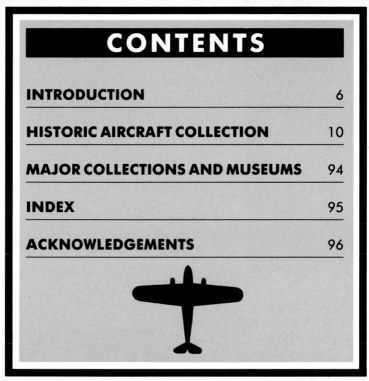

It would be hard to estimate the ratio of motor vehicles to aircraft (including all private, commercial and military types) that have been manufactured world wide. However, by all accounts, it will be many times in favour of the automotive industry.

When looking at the history of both forms of transport — and each in its own way has transformed the way in which we live — it is therefore somewhat surprising to find that in relative terms the number of preserved aircraft and aviation artifacts and memorabilia far outstrips anything the automotive industry can offer.

As to the reason why, who can tell? Maybe it's because aviation is more emotive; it could be that since in general many fewer examples of each aircraft type were built than cars, they tend to be individually recognized rather than being just one of a mass produced lot. Whatever the reason, aviation heritage is now recognized world wide as an integral part of twentieth century history as well as part of the history of individual countries.

It was the far-sighted views of a few that established the earliest aeronautical collections and so ensured the preservation of some of the finest aircraft types; men such as Samuel P Langley of the United States, the Englishman Sir Hiram Maxim and France's General Caquot were pioneers in this field. Langley started the Smithsonian's aeronautical collection as early as 1876 with the acquisition of a number of Chinese kites.

Above: The historic Wright Flyer can be seen at the National Air and Space Museum in Washington, DC.

Below: Airworthy World War II types at Duxford in Cambridgeshire, include the Morane-Saulnier MS315, DC-3 and B-17.

The early efforts did not all meet with success; some collections floundered due to a lack of support by their governments while others were partially destroyed as a result of wartime action. During the 1960s aircraft preservation continued to develop; both national and commercial museums flourished and aircraft preservation — and the practice of building replicas in the absence of the original — became an important aspect of the business.

Today, the preservation and use of vintage and historical aircraft can be summarized as follows: Museums may exhibit the original remains of an aircraft or a renovated model, either capable of flying or purely for display purposes. Privately owned aircraft may be used for private or pleasure flying, air shows, or air racing.

The museum category includes preservation societies, gate guardians (aircraft placed on display at the entrance to military bases), war memorials, and single-aircraft displays which might be found in locations as diverse as a playground or a hotel forecourt. It is nothing short of miraculous just what can be restored to flying — let alone display — condition. Given enough care and money, anything can be rebuilt.

However, it does raise the question of how much of the original aircraft is needed to ensure the result is not classed as a replica rather than an original. This is not to belittle the work of the aircraft engineers — both professional and amateur — who have produced superb replica aircraft over the years, distinguishable from the real thing only by close inspection. A number of replicas are museum pieces in their own right, including early examples of the Wright Flyer and Rumpler Taube, for example. Aircraft do not have to be veteran to be historic and worthy of preservation.

Above: Lancaster, Spitfire, Hurricane and Mosquito in formation.

America's North American XB-70 Valkyrie only flew for four and a half years during the 1960s and was earmarked for the United States Air Force Museum at Wright Paterson Air Base before it was even part way through its test programme while Britain's BAC TSR–2 survives in the form of two examples which never even got to fly before the programme was cancelled.

There is an increasing trend to display equipment in panoramic settings and as such even aircraft in present day front-line service can be found in air museums — witness the Argentinian FMA Pucaras in Britain as a direct result of the Falklands conflict.

There are now some 700 museums and aircraft collections worldwide. While some specialize, others offer a broader interest, often combining other aspects. Either way, it can be said that they generally provide interest as well as education, even for those who thought they were not air-minded.

Below: The Apollo 15. Will space museums rival air museums in the future?

In order to paint the broadest possible picture of just how aviation heritage is preserved this book contains a wide selection of historic aircraft from different locations around the world. The selection is purely subjective but all are historically significant; if you were to ask any aviation historian to compile a list using the same parameters, you would get very different results, which is part of the joy of searching out the historic aviation locations wherever you visit.

WINGS OF FREEDOM AIR AND SPACE MUSEUM

OWNER/OPERATOR	:	United States Navy
ADDRESS	:	Willow Grove Naval Air Station, Willow Grove, Pennsylvania 19090, USA
LOCATION	:	15 miles (24 km) north of Philadelphia. Road – Route 611
ADMISSION	:	Exhibits on display alongside boundary fence
FURTHER INFO	:	The airfield is an important US Navy and Marine reserve base.

Below: The Kawanishi NI KI can also be seen at the Wings of Freedom Air and Space Museum.

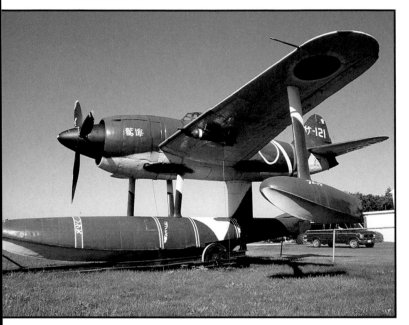

The most unusual aircraft can often be found where least expected. The US Naval Air Station at Willow Grove, Pennsylvania, offers many gems in its 'Wings of Freedom' collection, including a Japanese World War II Kawanishi N1K1 Shiden 'George' floatplane, complete with genuine bullet holes! The collection's unusual Messerschmitt Me262B-1A – a dual-control training version of Germany's second and most successful jet aircraft of World War II – keeps company with a rare beast, an Italian-built Arado Ar.196A-3 twin-float reconnaissance aircraft.

Probably the most successful seaplane operated by the German Navy's air forces during World War II, the Ar.196 was also used for light bombing and submarine hunting; two of these aircraft were instrumental in the capture of the British submarine HMS *Seal*. The Ar.196 warrants an entry in the record books if only because, as a warship-based aircraft, it took part in every naval operation of the war. In addition to its use on capital ships it became just as important in a coastal-based role.

Of 526 built, GA+DX is one of only three known survivors. Used as a spotter aircraft aboard the infamous German cruiser *Prince Eugen* during its raiding trips, the aircraft was captured intact aboard the ship and taken to Philadelphia as war spoils.

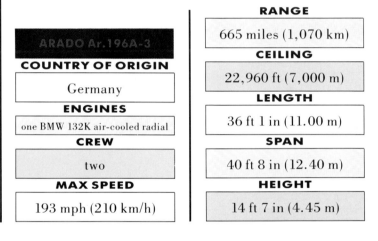

ARADO Ar.196A-3		
COUNTRY OF ORIGIN		**RANGE**
Germany		665 miles (1,070 km)
ENGINES		**CEILING**
one BMW 132K air-cooled radial		22,960 ft (7,000 m)
CREW		**LENGTH**
two		36 ft 1 in (11.00 m)
MAX SPEED		**SPAN**
193 mph (210 km/h)		40 ft 8 in (12.40 m)
		HEIGHT
		14 ft 7 in (4.45 m)

he success of the Avro Tutor as the RAF's standard trainer (replacing the immortal Avro 504) led the company to produce a version specifically for the civil market. Basically a scaled down Tutor, the Cadet first flew in 1931, and among the customers was the Portuguese Air Force. Two further variants appeared in 1934 and 1935, the latter also finding a military customer in the Royal Australian Air Force who ordered 34 machines.

The Tutor family were very popular aeroplanes and became well known to the British public in particular. As well as performing at the inter-war Hendon Air Displays, Tutors also joined Sir Alan Cobham's 'Flying Circus' to South Africa in 1932-33.

From a production run of 394 aircraft, just one Tutor remains today which is with the Shuttleworth Collection and in flying condition. The Cadet has fared a little better with two examples in Ireland, and one each in the UK, Portugal and Australia.

The Australian example, VH-PRT, is with the Drages Historical Aircraft Museum in Victoria, founded by Joe Drage in 1970. Some ten years later, the museum was purchased by Wangaratta City Council as a tourist attraction, Joe Drage staying on as manager.

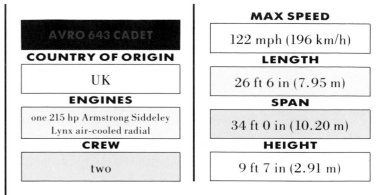

AVRO 643 CADET	
COUNTRY OF ORIGIN	**MAX SPEED**
UK	122 mph (196 km/h)
ENGINES	**LENGTH**
one 215 hp Armstrong Siddeley Lynx air-cooled radial	26 ft 6 in (7.95 m)
CREW	**SPAN**
two	34 ft 0 in (10.20 m)
	HEIGHT
	9 ft 7 in (2.91 m)

DRAGE'S AIRWORLD	
OWNER/OPERATOR :	Wangaratta City Council
ADDRESS :	Wangaratta Airfield, Wangaratta, Victoria, Australia
LOCATION :	Approx. 120 miles (190 km) NE of Melbourne
ADMISSION :	Daily 1000-1700
FURTHER INFO :	Joe Drage, who originally established the collection as a private venture, remains as manager of this now municipally owned contender as the most important collection of flying vintage civil aircraft in the southern hemisphere.

Out of the failure of the Avro Manchester bomber came the outstanding success of the Lancaster, arguably the greatest bomber of World War II. A twin-engined design, the Manchester suffered from development problems with its Rolls-Royce Vulture engines. The foresight of Avro's chief designer, Roy Chadwick, led to a developed airframe which would be powered by four Rolls-Royce Merlins — at that time in short supply, as it powered the Spitfire and Hurricane fighters. The redesigned aircraft was an immediate success and 7,377 machines were produced between October 1941 and the end of production in 1946, including 403 built by Victory Aircraft in Canada.

An initial bomb load of 4,000 lb (1,818 kg) increased through development and culminated with the famous 22,000 lb (1,000 kg) Grand Slam bomb designed by Barnes Wallis for destroying Germany's U-boat pens. The most famous operation involving Lancasters was by 617 (Dam Busters) Squadron RAF when they attacked three German dams in May 1943 with devastating effect.

Although not quite the hardest-working example of the type, R5868 survived 137 missions over enemy territory. Allocated to 83 Squadron, RAF with the code OL-Q, it made its first 'Op' on 8 July 1942 and survived the war to end its flying days with 467 (RAF) Squadron on 23 April 1945.

ROYAL AIR FORCE MUSEUM COLLECTION
BOMBER COMMAND MUSEUM

OWNER/OPERATOR	:	Royal Air Force
ADDRESS	:	Hendon, London NW9 5LL
LOCATION	:	9 miles northwest of London. Road – near to the A5
ADMISSION	:	Monday-Saturday 1000-1800, Sunday 1400-1800
FURTHER INFO	:	The historic aerodrome of Hendon is also the site of the Royal Air Force Museum and the Battle of Britain Museum.

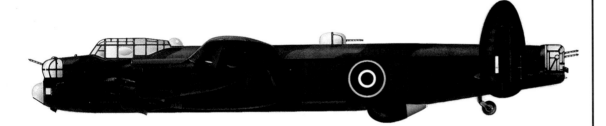

AVRO 683 LANCASTER I

COUNTRY OF ORIGIN
UK

ENGINES
four 1,460 hp Rolls-Royce Merlin XX air-cooled inline

CREW
Seven

MAX SPEED
287 mph (462 km/h)

RANGE
1,660 miles (2,675 km)

CEILING
24,500 ft (7,500 m)

LENGTH
69 ft 6 in (21.18 m)

SPAN
102 ft 0 in (31.09 m)

HEIGHT
20 ft 0 in (6.10 m)

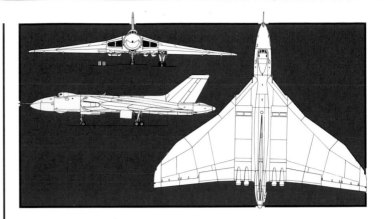

n the twilight years of their life, 26 years after the type entered service with the Royal Air Force, Avro Vulcans bombed the Falkland Islands airport of Port Stanley, so recording the first aggressive use of the aircraft in their long career.

The Vulcan was one of the three strategic 'V' bombers, ordered by the Royal Air Force in the immediate postwar years, as Britain's airborne nuclear deterrent, alongside the earlier Vickers Valiant and the Handley Page Victor. Initially designed to operate at high altitude, it carried the Blue Steel 'stand off' nuclear bomb. The Vulcan was later modified to undertake a tactical low-level role which it achieved with similar success.

The Vulcan is unmistakable owing to its unique delta wing, tested on a series of special development aircraft, also built by Avro. Its superb flight characteristics were enhanced by progressive improvements to the wing design, structural improvements and more powerful engines.

In their initial high-level role, all three 'V' bombers (so called because they each had a swept-back wing leading edge) were painted in an all-white 'anti-flash' colour scheme. The Vulcans later appeared in various camouflage schemes as they adopted new roles, and the few remaining aircraft from the production run of about 100 are displayed in their later colours.

The sole exception is XM603 which was acquired by a group of enthusiasts from the factory at Woodford, Manchester where it was originally built. Some of the group worked on the original airframe. Although not available for public display, except during the annual Royal Air Forces Association air display when the factory gates are thrown open, the aircraft was to have been restored to flying condition. This will not now happen, but XM603 will remain as a memorial to a superb design.

BRITISH AEROSPACE PLC

OWNER/OPERATOR	:	British Aerospace Avro Aircraft Restoration Society
ADDRESS	:	Woodford, Cheshire, UK
LOCATION	:	10 miles (16 km) south of Manchester city centre
ADMISSION	:	Not on public view, except during Woodford Air Show
FURTHER INFO	:	Contact Harry Holmes, British Aerospace PLC, Woodford, Cheshire SK7 1AR.

Below: The Avro Vulcan is also on display at the Strategic Air Command Museum in Nebraska.

AVRO VULCAN B.2		
COUNTRY OF ORIGIN	**RANGE**	
UK	4,000 miles (6,440 km)	
ENGINES	**CEILING**	
four 20,000 lb st (9,072 kg s t) Bristol Siddeley Olympus 201 turbojets	60,000 ft (18,290 m)	
CREW	**LENGTH**	
five	99 ft 11 in (30.45 m)	
MAX SPEED	**SPAN**	
635 mph (1,016 kph) (Mach 0.96 at 40,000 ft (12,400 m))	111 ft 0 in (33.83 m)	
	HEIGHT	
	27 ft 2 in (8.28 m)	

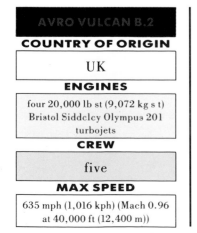

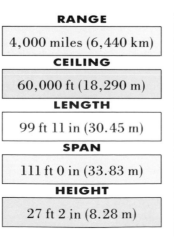

AVRO CANADA CF-100 CANUCK	
COUNTRY OF ORIGIN	
Canada	
ENGINES	
2 × 7,000 lb thrust Avro Orenda 11 turbojets	
CREW	
two	
MAX SPEED	
650 mph (1,040 km/h)	
RANGE	
1,700 miles (2,720 km)	
CEILING	
45,000 ft (13,950 m)	
LENGTH	
54 ft 2 in (16.53 m)	
SPAN	
58 ft 5 in (17.81 m)	
HEIGHT	
10 ft 7 in (3.30 m)	

HAMILTON CIVIC AIRPORT

OWNER/OPERATOR	:	Royal Canadian Air Force Club
ADDRESS	:	Hamilton Civil Airport, Mount Hope, Ontario, Canada L0R 1W0
LOCATION	:	8 miles south of Hamilton. Road – off Route 6
ADMISSION	:	On public view
FURTHER INFO	:	Hamilton Civic Airport is the home of the Canadian Warplane Heritage – one of the major military aircraft collections in North America.

The second largest country in the world and bounded by water on three sides, Canada has a unique air defence fighter requirement because of the extended range missions that are required.

Following the end of World War II, and with the development of its own aircraft industry (mainly through subsidiary companies set up by UK manufacturers), the Canadian government issued a request for an indigenous design to meet its requirements for the jet age.

The competition for a two-seat all-weather fighter was won by Avro Canada with a design somewhat resembling the English Electric Canberra. The CF-100 Canuck became the first aircraft wholly designed and built in Canada. Furthermore, the production versions were all powered by Canadian-built Orenda turbojets.

The first production variant, the Mk3, carried eight 0.5 in machine guns in a ventral pack, while the improved Mk4 had an all-rocket armament and enhanced radar. The final production was the Mk5 which was also supplied to the Belgian Air Force; an example is on display at the Royal Army Museum in Brussels. Although production ended in December 1958 after 692 examples had been built, the type remained in RCAF service for a further 30 years, ending its days on special duties.

At least nine Canucks survive in Canada as gate guardians and museum exhibits.

Two examples of the Avro Canada Canuck: *above*, at the Royal Army Museum in Brussels and *left*, at Hamilton Civic Airport, Hamilton, Ontario

BRITISH AIRCRAFT CORPORATION/ AEROSPATIALE CONCORDE

COUNTRY OF ORIGIN
UK/France

ENGINES
four 38,050 lb st Rolls-Royce Snecma Olympus 593

ACCOMMODATION
144 passengers (British Airways 100 passengers)

MAX SPEED
Mach 2.05

RANGE
3,550 nm (6,580 km)

CEILING
60,000 ft (18,290 m)

LENGTH
203 ft 9 in (62.10 m)

SPAN
83 ft 10 in (25.56 m)

HEIGHT
37 ft 5 in (11.40 m)

 ore than two decades after its first flight, Concorde remains the only successful supersonic transport aircraft in the world. The USSR managed to put their Tupolev TU-144 into service first, but it was soon withdrawn as a commercial failure, while the American Boeing 2707-300, which was to be larger and faster, was cancelled at design stage.

Two prototype and two pre-production aircraft were built which, despite the considerable interest initially shown by the world's major airlines, led to a production run of just 16 aircraft, seven each being purchased by British Airways and Air France. Both airlines started operations simultaneously on 21 January 1976, with services from London to Bahrain and Paris to Rio de Janeiro respectively.

The first prototype made its maiden flight on 2 March 1969 from Toulouse, France, followed by the British prototype, Concorde 002, on 9 April from Filton near Bristol. Twin assembly lines were set up at Toulouse and Filton while major airframe sections were made at other factories in the two countries.

Concorde 002 spent its life at the manufacturer's Flight Test Centre at Fairfield, where it was used for aerodynamic and engine development trials until its withdrawal from service in March 1976.

The aircraft was acquired by the Science Museum, who at that time had no suitable location where it could be displayed. The Fleet Air Arm Museum took the aircraft on loan and, stripped out and with its undercarriage locked down, 002 made its last flight to the museum's Yeovilton home base in the southwest of England.

Now situated in its own museum building, Concorde 002 is displayed with some of the research aircraft that were built as part of the research and development programme.

CONCORDE MUSEUM

OWNER/OPERATOR :		Science Museum/Royal Navy
ADDRESS	:	Royal Naval Air Station, Yeovilton, Ilchester, Somerset BA22 8HT
LOCATION	:	2 miles (3.2 km) east of Ilchester. Road – B3151
ADMISSION	:	Monday-Saturday 1000-1730, Sunday 1230-1730
FURTHER INFO	:	The Concorde Museum is independent to the Fleet Air Arm Museum and requires a separate entrance fee

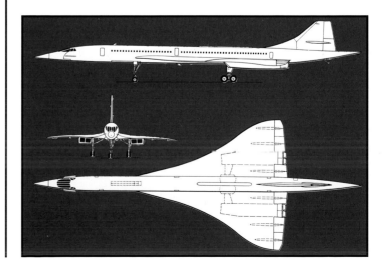

Many aircraft projects have been killed off at birth through political expediency, economic pressure or misguided advice. The Avro Canada Arrow Interceptor was one such project, cancelled in 1959 in the belief that all future aerial defence would be undertaken by ground-launched missiles.

Under a heavy cloud of uncertainty, the British Aircraft Corporation TSR.2 made its maiden flight in September 1964. Having completed just 24 flights, the prototype was grounded and the project cancelled in April 1965. None of the other aircraft near completion on the production line were ever to fly.

The TSR.2 (the initials stood for tactical strike and reconnaissance) was a truly revolutionary design and, had it not been cancelled, would still have been a front-line aircraft more than two decades later. Apart from its remarkable performance, its advanced avionics were far superior to any other systems available at that time. The determination of the UK government to see the end of the project meant that the manufacturers were instructed to destroy all 17 of the development aircraft then on the final production line, together with the production jigs, so that the project could not be revived at a later date.

Three airframes survived. One went ot a gunnery range for target practice, while a second found its way to the Imperial War Museum's collection at Duxford near Cambridge. The third example, which never took to the air, found shelter with the RAF's Historic Aircraft collection.

Above: The TSR.2 at the Imperial War Museum, Duxford, Cambridgeshire.

BRITISH AIRCRAFT CORPORATION TSR.2
COUNTRY OF ORIGIN
UK
ENGINES
two 30,610 lb st (13,885 kg st) Bristol Siddeley Olympus 320 turbojets
CREW
two
MAX SPEED
1,360 mph (2,185 km/h)
RANGE
2,300 miles (3,706 km)
CEILING
60,000 ft (18,290 m)
LENGTH
89 ft 0 in (27.13 m)
SPAN
37 ft 0 in (11.28 m)
HEIGHT
24 ft 0 in (7.32 m)

ROYAL AIR FORCE MUSEUM COLLECTION AEROSPACE MUSEUM	
OWNER/OPERATOR :	Royal Air Force Museum Collection
ADDRESS :	RAF Cosford, Wolverhampton, West Midlands, WV7 3EX
LOCATION :	8 miles northwest of Wolverhampton. Road – off the A41
ADMISSION :	April-October 1000-1600 daily; November-March 1000-1800 Monday-Friday
FURTHER INFO :	As well as being a major part of the Royal Air Force Museum Collection, Cosford is also home to the British Airways collection of airliners used by BA and its predecessors since 1945.

he United States Army Air Force and the Royal Air Force held different views on the most effective way strategically to attack Germany during World War II. The British had developed night bombing techniques, and therefore designed their bombers to carry less defensive armament than their US counterparts, who had elected for daylight bombing with its greater risk of fighter attack.

As such, the standard USAAF bomber of the war became the Boeing B-17 Fortress, so named because it bristled with machine guns. The later models were fitted with twin 0.5-inch Brownings in chin, dorsal, ball and tail turrets, plus two in nose sockets, another in the radio compartment and one in each waist position.

Boeing first flew their B-17 in July 1935, developed to meet a United States Army Air Corps requirement, using experience gained with their Model 247 transport. While the first variants to see service in Europe were found somewhat lacking, the re-designed B-17E, which featured a new rear section to improve high altitude performance, and subsequent models became the mainstay of the United States Army Eighth Air Force.

To ease production difficulties, most of the 12,731 examples built came from Lockheed and Douglas factories. A somewhat surprisingly large number of B-17s still exist. Many are in flying condition, either as museum pieces or, even now, with commercial operators for uses such as water-bombing forest fires.

The Mud Island leisure complex at Memphis, Tennessee proudly displays B-17F *Memphis Belle*, the best-known US bomber of World War II, and star of the recent Steven Spielberg film of the same name.

Right: The Boeing B-17 Fortress at Mud Island.

Below: At the Confederate Air Force Base in Mesa, Arizona.

MUD ISLAND LEISURE COMPLEX	
OWNER/OPERATOR :	Memphis City
ADDRESS :	125 North Front Street, Memphis, Tennessee 38103
LOCATION :	In the western part of the city
ADMISSION :	April-October 1000-2200 daily; November, December, March 1000-1700 daily
FURTHER INFO :	*Memphis Belle* is situated in its own specially constructed pavilion.

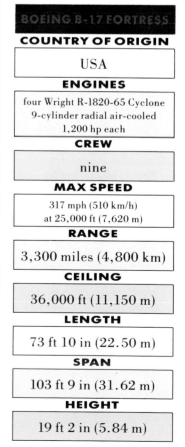

BOEING B-17 FORTRESS
COUNTRY OF ORIGIN
USA
ENGINES
four Wright R-1820-65 Cyclone 9-cylinder radial air-cooled 1,200 hp each
CREW
nine
MAX SPEED
317 mph (510 km/h) at 25,000 ft (7,620 m)
RANGE
3,300 miles (4,800 km)
CEILING
36,000 ft (11,150 m)
LENGTH
73 ft 10 in (22.50 m)
SPAN
103 ft 9 in (31.62 m)
HEIGHT
19 ft 2 in (5.84 m)

BOEING B-29-45-MO SUPERFORTRESS	
COUNTRY OF ORIGIN	
USA	
ENGINES	
four 2,200 hp Wright Cyclone air-cooled radial	
CREW	
ten	
MAX SPEED	
358 mph (576 km/h)	
RANGE	
4,100 miles (6,600 km)	
CEILING	
31,850 ft (9,700 m)	
LENGTH	
99 ft 0 in (30.18 m)	
SPAN	
141 ft 3 in (43.05 m)	
HEIGHT	
29 ft 7 in (9.02 m)	

There is a touch of irony that the aircraft which unleashed the holocaust of the world's first atomic bomb dropped in anger ended up near-derelict at the end of a runway on a USAF base. The irony goes further; just as the Japanese city of Hiroshima was rebuilt following that fateful attack on 6 August 1945, the Boeing B-29 Superfortress *Enola Gay* was rescued from its fate of decay to be restored for permanent display.

Piloted by Col Paul W Tibbets, Jr, *Enola Gay* entered the history books at 8.15 am on 6 August 1945, when the six-ton (6,096 kg) atomic bomb nicknamed 'Little Boy' was released over Hiroshima. Fifty seconds later, the bomb exploded with the force of 20,000 tons (20,400 tonnes) of TNT, destroying 4.7 square miles (7.5 km^2) of the city centre, leaving 71,379 dead and over 68,000 injured.

Three days after the Hiroshima attack, a sister ship, *Bock's Car,* captained by Lt Col Charles W Sweeney, dropped the second operational atomic bomb on the city of Nagasaki. The two attacks quickly brought an end to the Second World War with the Japanese officially surrendering on 2 September 1945.

Today, *Enola Gay* is in the care of the world-renowned Smithsonian Institution's National Air and Space Museum. It is presently at the museum's Paul E Garber Facility, where it is being restored to display condition.

The museum is possibly the world's most important aircraft collection. Many of its most famous exhibits, including the Wright Flyer and Lindbergh's *Spirit of St Louis* can be seen at the Smithsonian Institution in Washington DC.

NATIONAL AIR AND SPACE MUSEUM		
OWNER/OPERATOR	:	Smithsonian Institution
ADDRESS	:	Paul E Garber Facility, Silver Hill Road, Suitland, Maryland
LOCATION	:	6 miles (9.6 km) southeast of Washington DC
ADMISSION	:	Tours by appointment Monday-Friday 1000; Saturday & Sunday 1000 & 1300
FURTHER INFO	:	The Garber Facility is the outstation to the main museum and contains the restoration workshops. Some 140 aircraft are on display.

BOEING KC-97G STRATOFREIGHTER

COUNTRY OF ORIGIN
USA

ENGINES
4 × 3,500 hp Pratt & Whitney R4360-75 piston engines

CREW
5 plus 96 troops or up to 68,500 lb cargo

MAX SPEED
350 mph (560 km/h)

RANGE
4,300 miles (6,888 km) at 300 mph (480 km/h) at 25,000 ft (7,625 m)

CEILING
35,000 ft (10,675 m)

LENGTH
117 ft 5 in (35.7 m)

SPAN
141 ft 3 in (43.75 m)

HEIGHT
38 ft 3 in (11.86 m)

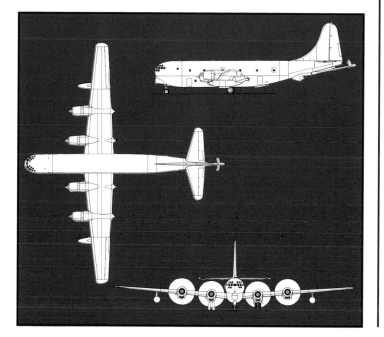

Boeing's policy of developing existing technology continued with the first flight of its XC-97 prototype on 15 November 1944 in response to a military requirement issued in 1942 for a large transport aircraft. Although the wing platform and tail assembly were adapted from the B-29, the completely new 'double bubble' twin deck fuselage, which gave the aircraft its massive carrying capability, made the C-97 unmistakable.

The first variant, a pure freighter, was followed by personnel transport, command post and in-flight refuelling tanker (KC-97) versions, the latter fitted with 'flying boom' equipment. In total, production ran to 888 military machines.

Boeing developed a purely civil version of the C-97, designated the Model 377 Stratocruiser, with accommodation for up to 100 passengers on long-haul flights. Fifty-five production aircraft followed the prototype's first flight in July 1947. They saw service with five US airlines, including Pan American, and BOAC, who operated them until May 1959.

Despite their size, over 30 examples of the C-97 Stratofreighter remain in a preserved state worldwide, including the KC-97G tanker variant at Grissom Air Force Base Heritage Museum, Indiana.

The base adopted its present name in May 1968 in memory of Col Virgil I Grissom, who died in a flash fire aboard an Apollo capsule during a ground test at Cape Kennedy in 1967.

GRISSOM AIR FORCE BASE HERITAGE MUSEUM

OWNER/OPERATOR :	United States Air Force	
ADDRESS :	305 Arefw, Grissom Air Force Base, Indiana 46971	
LOCATION :	7 miles south of Pen. Road – Route 31	
ADMISSION :	Prior permission only	
FURTHER INFO :	The types on display include many which have operated from the base.	

Following their established tradition of producing highly successful heavy bombers, Boeing approached the task of their first jet-powered derivative as soon as a suitable powerplant was available.

Meanwhile, although originally designed as a piston-engined bomber, the North American B-45 Tornado became the first four-engined jet aircraft to fly in the United States when it took to the air in March 1947. Just 139 were produced, and the last reconnaissance version was finally withdrawn in 1958. In comparison, some 1,800 Boeing B-47 Stratojets were produced from the prototype of 1947 to the final production aircraft of 1957 and remained in service until the mid 1960s.

The first succesful long-range jet bomber, the B-47 also saw service in photo-reconnaissance and weather research roles, in addition to specialist uses as a missile target drone, crew trainer and special trials platform. Powered by six General Electric J47s, the B-47 was manufactured by Douglas at Tulsa and Lockheed at Marietta as well as Boeing at Wichita. With its distinctive cigar-shaped fuselage and narrow highly swept-back wings, it was a familiar sight in the skies over Europe, Japan and northern Canada, as well as the United States.

As headquarters of the Strategic Air Command, it is natural that Offutt Air Force Base features a B-47 within its comprehensive collection of strategic bombers used by SAC.

BOEING B-47E STRATOJET	STRATEGIC AIR COMMAND MUSEUM	
COUNTRY OF ORIGIN	**OWNER/OPERATOR** :	United States Air Force
USA	**ADDRESS** :	2510 Clay Street, Belleville, Nebraska 68005
ENGINES	**LOCATION** :	10 miles south of Omaha. Road – Interstate 80
six General Electric J47-GE-25 turbojets, 6,000 lb (2,721 kg) thrust each	**ADMISSION** :	Daily 0800 -1700
CREW	**FURTHER INFO** :	Among the types exhibited, the bombers represent most types used by SAC from the B-17 Fortress to the B-58 Hustler.
three		

Inset Bottom Left: The B-47E on display at Plattsburgh Military Museum, New York.

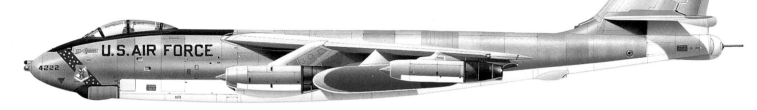

MAX SPEED
606 mph (975 km/h) at 16,300 ft (4,968 m)
RANGE
4,000 miles (6,435 km)
CEILING
40,500 ft (12,345 m)
LENGTH
109 ft 10 in (33.4 7 m)
SPAN
116 ft (35.35 m)
HEIGHT
27 ft 11 in (8.50 m)

he development of aircraft design between the start of World War I in 1914, and the appearance of the later types in 1917 and 1918, was truly dramatic. Many superb designs had been introduced by the warring nations, but the appearance of the Bristol Fighter firmly put the balance of air power in the laps of the Allied forces.

Variously described as 'one of the classic aircraft of World War I', and 'a fighter which can be considered one of the very best of the war' among many other accolades, the two-seat Bristol F.2 was designed in March 1916 by Captain Frank S Barnwell who, dissatisfied with existing Allied types, wanted to produce a fighter to match the German types of the time.

The F.2 met with disaster on its first mission when all six air-craft were engaged and shot down by a similar number of Albatross D.IIIs, with the loss of the all 12 airmen. The fault, however, was found to be not with the aircraft, but the fact that the fliers had not been trained in the use of a forward firing weapon which the F.2 carried in addition to the rear gun.

Together with better trained aircrew, the impoved F.2B, with a more powerful engine and greater range, took over the skies during the later phases of the war. It remained in RAF service until as late as 1932, being used for army co-operation duties.

Of the 5,308 machines produced, just four remain, all in the UK. One is still airworthy with the Shuttleworth Collection, who have a policy of maintaining their historic aircraft in flying condition wherever possible.

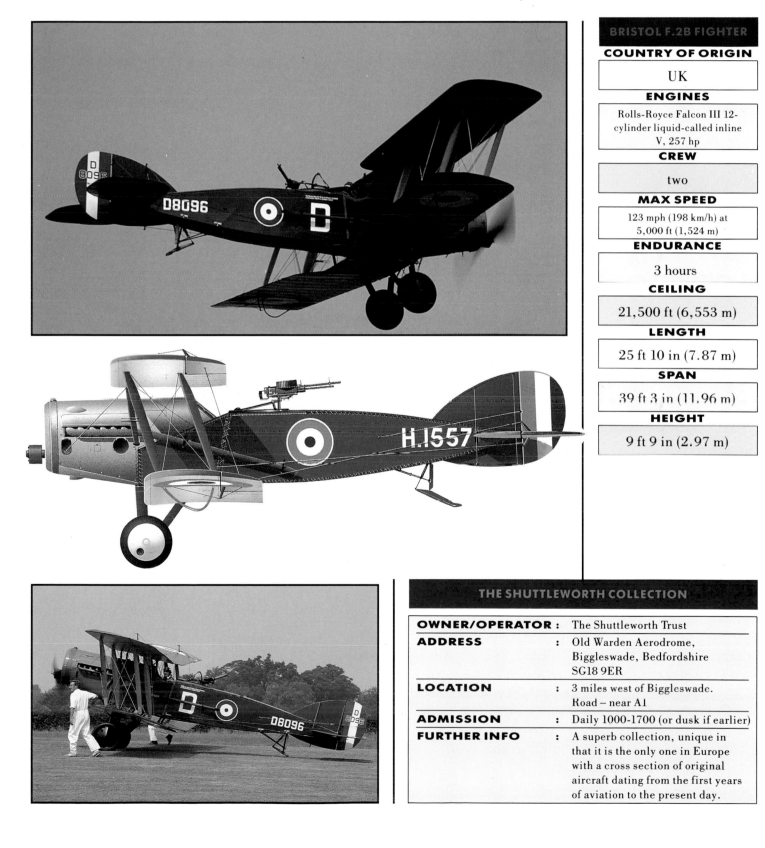

BRISTOL F.2B FIGHTER	
COUNTRY OF ORIGIN	
UK	
ENGINES	
Rolls-Royce Falcon III 12-cylinder liquid-called inline V, 257 hp	
CREW	
two	
MAX SPEED	
123 mph (198 km/h) at 5,000 ft (1,524 m)	
ENDURANCE	
3 hours	
CEILING	
21,500 ft (6,553 m)	
LENGTH	
25 ft 10 in (7.87 m)	
SPAN	
39 ft 3 in (11.96 m)	
HEIGHT	
9 ft 9 in (2.97 m)	

THE SHUTTLEWORTH COLLECTION		
OWNER/OPERATOR	:	The Shuttleworth Trust
ADDRESS	:	Old Warden Aerodrome, Biggleswade, Bedfordshire SG18 9ER
LOCATION	:	3 miles west of Biggleswade. Road – near A1
ADMISSION	:	Daily 1000-1700 (or dusk if earlier)
FURTHER INFO	:	A superb collection, unique in that it is the only one in Europe with a cross section of original aircraft dating from the first years of aviation to the present day.

A classic two-seat aerobatic trainer, the Bucker Bu131 Jungmann was designed, in the mid 1930s, for use by flying schools. Not surprisingly, following the first flight of the type in 1934, large numbers were ordered for the Luftsportverband, which naturally led to additional orders for the later, more powerful, versions.

With the outbreak of hostilities, the Jungmann was widely used by the Luftwaffe for both training and general utility purposes, with over 4,000 examples being produced in Germany.

Meanwhile, a single-seat advanced aerobatic trainer derivative, the Bu133 Jungmeister, was introduced in 1935. Like its big brother, the Jungmann, the Jungmeister was built under licence in Switzerland, Spain and other countries, while exports went much further afield. Illustrating the popularity of the types, following an initial production run of 150 Jungmanns by CASA, the Spanish company reopened the line in 1956 to produce a further 50 examples. These aircraft are so popular for their aerobatic qualities that many are still flying on both sides of the Atlantic, although some have been re-engined to provide enhanced performance.

Others grace museum collections such as the ex-Swiss Air Force Bu131B which is attractively displayed within the terminal buildings at Zurich Airport.

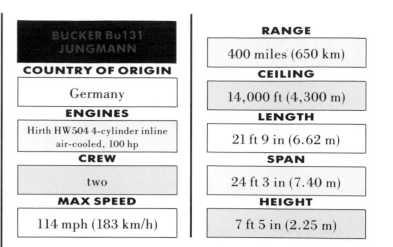

BUCKER Bu131 JUNGMANN		
COUNTRY OF ORIGIN		**RANGE**
Germany		400 miles (650 km)
ENGINES		**CEILING**
Hirth HW504 4-cylinder inline air-cooled, 100 hp		14,000 ft (4,300 m)
		LENGTH
		21 ft 9 in (6.62 m)
CREW		**SPAN**
two		24 ft 3 in (7.40 m)
MAX SPEED		**HEIGHT**
114 mph (183 km/h)		7 ft 5 in (2.25 m)

FLUGHAFEN ZURICH

OWNER/OPERATOR	:	Flughafen Zurich
ADDRESS	:	Flughafen Zurich, Kloten, Switzerland
LOCATION	:	In Terminal B
ADMISSION	:	When terminal building is open
FURTHER INFO	:	There are three aircraft on view in the shopping area.

Top: The Bucker BU131 Jungmann.
Bottom: The Bucker BU133 Jungmeister.

oteworthy for its remarkable range of over 3,000 miles, as well as for its toughness and reliability, the Catalina had a distinguished service record in many theatres during World War II, operating mainly in the anti-submarine and convoy escort roles. The prototype, designated XP3Y-1, flew in 1935, and after flight testing established a distance record of 3,443 miles. Sixty production aircraft were initially ordered by the US Navy, which eventually received 1,196 examples of the Catalina flying boat and 944 of the amphibious version, which appeared in 1940 and which was fitted with a tricycle undercarriage.

The name Catalina was first used by the RAF, which in 1939 ordered an initial batch of 50 for service with Coastal Command on the North Atlantic convoy routes. Total British orders rose to 650 before the end of the war. Three RAF Catalina pilots were awarded the Victoria Cross for gallantry in action against German U-Boats.

In addition to the US Navy and the RAF, Catalinas were also ordered by Australia, Canada, France and the Netherlands East Indies. Several hundred were also built in the Soviet Union, where the aircraft was designated GST. Total production of the Catalina in the USA and Canada was 3,290.

After the war, many surplus Catalinas were sold off to countries such as Argentina, Brazil, Chile, Ecuador, Mexico, Nationalist China, Dominica, Indonesia and Peru, where they were often used as commercial transports as well as maritime patrol aircraft. The type remained in use in its commercial role well into the 1960s in such areas as the Amazon basin and among the island groups of South-East Asia and Australasia.

CONFEDERATE AIR FORCE (PACIFIC WING)

OWNER/OPERATOR :		Confederate Air Force
ADDRESS	:	51 Las Palomas, Orinda, California 94563
LOCATION	:	Vacaville Airport, 40 miles northeast of San Franciso. Road – Interstate 80
ADMISSION	:	Prior permission only
FURTHER INFO	:	The wing also maintains an AT-6D Texan

CONSOLIDATED PBY-5A CATALINA

COUNTRY OF ORIGIN	
USA	
ENGINES	
two Pratt & Whitney R-1830-82 twin wasp 14-cylinder radial air-cooled, 1,200 hp each	
CREW	
seven to nine	
MAX SPEED	
175 mph (281 km/h) at 7,000 ft (2,135 m)	
RANGE	
2,350 miles (3,780 km)	
CEILING	
18,100 ft (5,520 m)	
LENGTH	
63ft 10 in (19.45 m)	
SPAN	
104 ft 0 in (31.70 m)	
HEIGHT	
20 ft 2 in (6.14 m)	

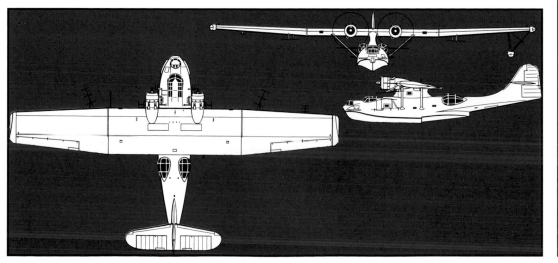

Top: The Catalina at the Confederate Air Force Wing, and *above left*, the example held by 'Plane Sailing', Duxford, Cambridgeshire.

lthough basically a conventional design for the time, the Convair B-36 strategic bomber contained many unusual features. These included six radial engines buried in the wing trailing edges in pusher configuration, together with twin-podded jet engines under each wing. The fuselage contained two pressurized compartments connected by an 80 ft (24.4 m) tunnel which incorporated a wheeled trolley.

The aircraft was produced in response to a US Army Air Force requirement for a large bomber that could carry a massive 10,000 lb (4,536 kg) bomb load over a distance of 10,000 miles (16,094 km) at a service ceiling of 35,000 ft (10,670 m). However, as the USSR began developing turbojet-powered fighters with greatly increased performance, Convair boosted the original B-36 six piston-engine design to include four General Electric J-47 jet engines which significantly increased both speed and altitude.

The B-36 did not see service in World War II, its development being delayed by other projects. It made its first flight in August 1946, and reached training units exactly one year later.

In addition to strategic bombing, they were widely used for strategic reconnaissance. Designated RB-36F and RB-36H, they carried 14 cameras in the forward bomb bay, including one with a 42 in (105 cm) focal length lens.

Although the mainstay of the Strategic Air Command's long range force throughout the 1950s, only four examples still exist. The sole remaining RB-36H can be found at the Chanute Air Force Base Collection in Illinois, where it can be compared directly with its immediate predecessors and successors.

Chanute AFB was named after the pioneer aviator Octave Chanute. It has been a technical training school since 1921, and remains as an active airfield.

CHANUTE AIR FORCE BASE COLLECTION

OWNER/OPERATOR	:	Chanute Technical Training Centre
ADDRESS	:	Chanute Air Force Base, Illinois 61868
LOCATION	:	South of Rantoul. Road – Route 45
ADMISSION	:	Tuesday-Thursday 1000-1500, Friday-Saturday 0900-1700
FURTHER INFO	:	Within the collection, the Thunderbirds Air Park honours the famous aerobatic display team and its predecessors.

The Convair can be seen at Chanute Air Force Base (below) as well as at the Strategic Air Command Museum, Nebraska (bottom).

CONVAIR RB-36H

COUNTRY OF ORIGIN	
USA	
ENGINES	
six Pratt & Whitney 3,800 hp Wasp Major radials and four General Electric 5,200 lb (2,364 kg) J-47 jet	
CREW	
fifteen	
MAX SPEED	
436 mph (702 km/h)	
RANGE	
10,000 miles (16,094 km)	
CEILING	
45,000 ft (72,450 m)	
LENGTH	
162 ft 1 in (50.22 m)	
SPAN	
230 ft 0 in (71.3 m)	
HEIGHT	
46 ft 9 in (14.49 m)	

The first jet fighter of French design to be ordered in quantity, the Dassault Ouragan first flew on 28 February 1949, powered by a licence-built Rolls-Royce Nene turbojet. 362 examples were ordered by the French Air Force, equipping four fighter wings in 1952. In 1953 the Indian Air Force placed an order for 71 aircraft, and in February 1957 13 more were shipped to India aboard the French aircraft carrier Dixmude. Named *Toofani* (Whirlwind) in Indian service, the Ouragan began to be replaced by the Mystère IV in 1958, but remained in service as an operational trainer until well into the 1960s.

The second overseas customer was the Israeli Air Force, which received an initial batch of Ouragans in November 1955. During the next two years the number of Ouragans supplied to Israel rose to 75. The aircraft saw action in the Arab-Israeli war of 1956 and proved capable of absorbing considerable battle damage, although they were distinctly inferior to the MiG-15s used by the Egyptian Air Force. As in India, the Ouragan was used for some years in the operational training role after being phased out of first-line service. In addition to its built-in armament of four 20 mm cannon, the Ouragan could carry a variety of bombs and rocket projectiles, and during the Arab-Israeli war it took part in some notable ground attack missions, particularly against the Egyptian 1st Armoured Division in Sinai. Rocket-firing Ouragans also disabled the Egyptian destroyer *Ibrahim el Awal*, which was captured by the Israeli Navy.

In 1975 Israel supplied 18 of her surviving Ouragans to El Salvador, which was still using them in the 1980s for ground-attack operations against left-wing guerrilla forces. Five of the Ouragans were destroyed in 1982 during a guerrilla raid on their base at Ilopango.

ABBEVILLE AIRFIELD		
OWNER/OPERATOR	:	Aero Club de la Somme
ADDRESS	:	Drucat, Abbeville 80, France
LOCATION	:	Outside the motel at the airfield
ADMISSION	:	Free access
FURTHER INFO	:	The well-weathered aircraft has been on display at the airport since at least 1967.

DASSAULT MD.450 OURAGAN			
COUNTRY OF ORIGIN		**RANGE**	
France		570 miles (920 km)	
ENGINES		**CEILING**	
Hispano-Suiza Nene 104B turbojet, 5,000 lb (2,270 kg) thrust		43,000 ft (13,000 m)	
		LENGTH	
		35 ft 3 in (10.74 m)	
CREW		**SPAN**	
one		43 ft 2 in (13.16 m)	
MAX SPEED		**HEIGHT**	
584 mph (940 km/h) at sea level		13 ft 7 in (4.14 m)	

Main picture: An example of the Ouragon at the Indian Air Force Museum in Palam.
Inset: The Ouragon at the Aeroclub de la Somme.

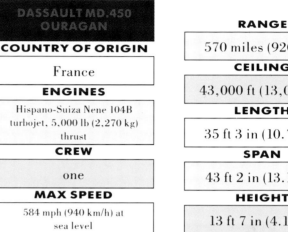

If the Avro 504 is considered the world's greatest training aircraft, then the de Havilland Tiger Moth must be a worthy runner-up. A descendant of the D.H.60 Moth, which revolutionized private flying in the 1920s, the Tiger Moth became the RAF's standard initial trainer during World War II.

From 1932 until 1947 it saw service with the RAF, who operated some 4,000 during the war. A further 3,000 examples were built under licence in Canada, Australia and New Zealand under the Commonwealth Air Training Scheme.

A fully aerobatic aircraft, the Tiger Moth was also used for blind flying instruction where the trainee pilot had to sit beneath a hood fitted over the rear cockpit and fly the aircraft solely on instruments. Following the end of hostilities, many Tiger Moths were put up for sale and flooded the civil market. Flying clubs, flying schools and individual pilots were keen to purchase surplus military machines and the type took on a new lease of life.

Sixty years after the prototype's first flight, the Tiger Moth is still revered by many aviation enthusiasts. Examples can be found in flying condition at airfields across the world, in addition to those which have found a home in a museum.

One such example is N39DH, which was painstakingly restored by Kurt Hofschneider of New Jersey. His 1939 machine, immaculately painted in the standard RAF training colour scheme of the time, can be seen at air shows across the USA and often wins the first prize for 'Concours d'Elegance'.

KURT HOFSCHNEIDER

OWNER/OPERATOR	:	Kurt Hofschneider
ADDRESS	:	Colonia, New Jersey
LOCATION	:	Alexandria, New Jersey
ADMISSION	:	On view at any reasonable time
FURTHER INFO	:	Kurt's Tiger Moth is included in this volume to represent the thousands of lovingly care-for vintage aircraft in private ownership throughout the world.

DE HAVILLAND D.H.82A TIGER MOTH

COUNTRY OF ORIGIN	**RANGE**
UK	300 miles (482 km)
ENGINES	**CEILING**
one 130 hp de Havilland Gypsy Major air-cooled inline	14,000 ft (4,267 km)
CREW	**LENGTH**
two	23 ft 11 in (7.29 m)
MAX SPEED	**SPAN**
	29 ft 4 in (8.94 m)
109 mph (176 km/h)	**HEIGHT**
	8 ft 9.5 in (2.66 m)

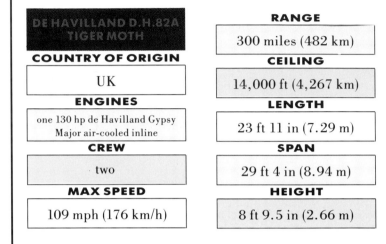

Following the tremendous success of their Gypsy Moth, the two-seat light aircraft which was developed from the earlier D.H.60 moth, de Havilland were hard put to find a successor.

The answer lay in the Hornet Moth which featured an enclosed cockpit with two seats side by side, like a coupe car. The first prototype took to the air in May 1934 and production began a year later.

The first Hornet Moths featured a tapered wing with rounded tips, copied from the larger D.H.86 airliner. However, although the design maximized performance, it caused a sharp wing drop at the stall and so a square-tipped wing was adopted.

As the D.H.87B, the Hornet Moth had an assured future. Not only were its flying qualities, which included high stability and a 40 mph (64.4 km/h) stall, excellent, a practical range of some 600 miles (966 km) with internal stowage for a couple of large suitcases and golf clubs made the design extremely attractive.

In the flying training role, the pupil no longer had to dress for an open cockpit, could converse with the instructor without using headphones and could watch what he was doing.

A further bonus was the price — £875 fully equipped.

Many Hornet Moths were impressed into war service with the RAF on communications duties. Twenty-four returned to civilian life afterwards and many of these are still flying, mainly in the British Isles.

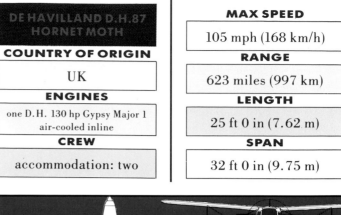

DE HAVILLAND D.H.87 HORNET MOTH	
COUNTRY OF ORIGIN	**MAX SPEED**
UK	105 mph (168 km/h)
ENGINES	**RANGE**
one D.H. 130 hp Gypsy Major 1 air-cooled inline	623 miles (997 km)
CREW	**LENGTH**
accommodation: two	25 ft 0 in (7.62 m)
	SPAN
	32 ft 0 in (9.75 m)

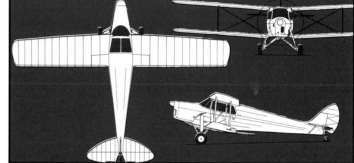

SOUTH AFRICAN AIR FORCE MUSEUM

OWNER/OPERATOR	:	South African Air Force
ADDRESS	:	Krugersdorp Road, Lanseria
LOCATION	:	Approx 30 miles (48 km; south west of Pretoria
ADMISSION	:	Contact base for details
FURTHER INFO	:	Lanseria Airport is the site of the museum's restoration and storage hangar.

The MacRobertson England to Australia air race of 1934 attracted considerable interest worldwide. In response to the challenge, Geoffrey de Havilland put his design team to work, even though the first prize was not financially rewarding.

The result was a dedicated twin-engined low-wing monoplane – the DH.88 Comet racer. The Comet – a name later to be attached to the world's first jet airliner – incorporated a number of novel features. It was the first British aircraft to combine a retractable undercarriage, split flaps and variable pitch propellers.

Three aircraft were ordered for the race. The first to fly, G-ACSR, took to the air for the first time on 8 September 1934, followed shortly by 'CSP and 'CSS in time for the start of the race from Mildenhall on 20 October. 'CSP was flown by Jim and Amy Mollison who had to retire en route at Allahabad, while in the lead, owing to engine trouble. 'CSS, entered by the managing director of London's Grosvenor House Hotel and flown by C W A Scott and Tom Campbell Black, won the race in a time of 70 hours, 54 minutes and 18 seconds, 20 hours ahead of the runner-up Douglas DC-2.

The third Comet, flown by Ken Waller and Owen Cathcart-Jones, was placed fourth with a time of 108 hours and 13 minutes. They immediately turned for home and arrived back at Lympne on 2 November, setting a new out-and-back record.

After the race, 'CSP was sold in Portugal, 'CSR went to France, while 'CSS was acquired by the Royal Aircraft Establishment, being presented to the Shuttleworth Collection in 1965 after many years in store.

Following ten years of static display, 'CSS was restored to flying condition. 'CSP was retrieved from Portugal in 1979 and is currently being restored at Staverton airport, between Gloucester and Cheltenham.

Right and below: The comet racer at the Shuttleworth collection.

DE HAVILLAND D.H.88 COMET	
COUNTRY OF ORIGIN	
UK	
ENGINES	
two de Havilland Gypsy Six R, 6-cylinder inline, air-cooled, 230 hp	
CREW	
two	
MAX SPEED	
237 mph (381 km/h)	
RANGE	
2,925 miles (4,707 km)	
CEILING	
19,000 ft (5,790 m)	
LENGTH	
29 ft 0 in (8.83 m)	
SPAN	
44 ft 0 in (13.41 m)	
HEIGHT	
10 ft 0 in (3.05 m)	

One of the lesser known of Geoffrey de Havilland's inter-war series of civil aircraft, the DH.90 Dragonfly was a five-seat light or executive transport developed from the more famous DH.84 Dragon. Apart from the fact that both were powered by a pair of 130 hp Gypsy Major engines, the two aircraft bore little resemblance to one another. The most notable feature about the Dragonfly was its fuselage, which was a wooden monocoque of extremely advanced design — incorporating, in fact, some of the technology that would later be used in the design of the RAF's celebrated Mosquito fighter-bomber. The DH.90's wings were sharply tapered, and in this respect it resembled another of the de Havilland airliner family, the DH.89 Dragon Rapide.

The DH.90 flew for the first time on 12 August 1935 and 66 examples were built over the next three years, mainly as executive transports. Most served with British companies, but a few found their way overseas. Some DH.90s sold to Canada were extensively modified for bush operations and were fitted with floats. Four of them became the original fleet of the Royal Canadian Mounted Police Air Division.

VINTAGE AIRCRAFT TEAM	
ADDRESS	: Cranfield Airfield, Bedford, UK
LOCATION	: 8 miles (13 km) south west of Bedford Road – Off the A421
ADMISSION	: The aircraft are situated on the airfield, which is open to the public every day of the week
FURTHER INFO	: At the time of publication, the Vintage Aircraft Team were preparing to move to a new location, near Leicester.

Right: The DH 90 at Cranfield.
Below: The DH 84 Dragon at the Wagon to Wings Air Museum, Morgan Hill, California.

DE HAVILLAND D.H.90 DRAGONFLY		
COUNTRY OF ORIGIN		
UK		
ENGINES		
two 130 hp D.H. Gypsy Major 1		
CREW		
FIVE		
MAX SPEED		
125 mph (200 km/h)		
RANGE		
900 miles (1,449 km)		
CEILING		
18,100 ft (5,611 m)		
LENGTH		
31 ft 8 in (9.5 m)		
SPAN		
43 ft 0 in (13.11 m)		
HEIGHT		
9 ft 2 in (2.81 m)		

An all-wooden unarmed bomber, powered by two Rolls-Royce Merlin engines would have appeared to have stood little chance of success in 1939. Merlin engines were in short supply and badly needed to power Spitfire and Hurricane fighters.

Geoffrey de Havilland, however, had confidence in his company's design, owing to the success of the Comet racer and the Albatross airliner, and he developed the project as a private venture, even though the Air Ministry showed little interest. Less than 11 months elapsed between the eventual Ministry go-ahead and the first flight of the Mosquito prototype on 25 November 1940. The performance surprised even de Havilland's engineers and the Mosquito remained the world's fastest operational aircraft until the introduction of jet aircraft some two and a half years later.

Built in the UK, Australia and Canada, 7,718 aircraft were produced in 40 different marks. As well as the original bomber design, Mosquitos were also produced as night fighters, fighter bombers, photo reconnaissance and trainers while some were converted for target towing duties. The original prototype, designed and built at Salisbury Hall, a 17th-century house near de Havilland's factory, was flown in a distinctive all-yellow colour scheme so that British anti-aircraft gunners would recognize the unfamiliar shape.

It not only survived the war but also the type's final withdrawal from RAF service in 1963. Meanwhile, in 1959, the owner of Salisbury Hall had acquired the aircraft and, with the help of enthusiasts, has since built up an impressive museum of de Havilland aircraft and engines and memorabilia.

THE MOSQUITO AIRCRAFT MUSEUM		
ADDRESS	:	Salisbury Hall, London Colney, St Albans, Hertfordshire AL2 1BU
LOCATION	:	5 miles south of St Albans. Road – off M25 Junction 22
ADMISSION	:	Easter-September 1400-1800 (Sundays) 1030-1230, 1400-1730 (Bank Holidays)
FURTHER INFO	:	Britain's oldest aircraft museum is in the grounds of the seventeenth-century Salisbury Hall and is dedicated to preserving both aircraft and engines of de Havilland.

Main picture: At the Mosquito Aircraft Museum.
Inset: The Mosquito at Hamilton Airforce Base, Ontario.

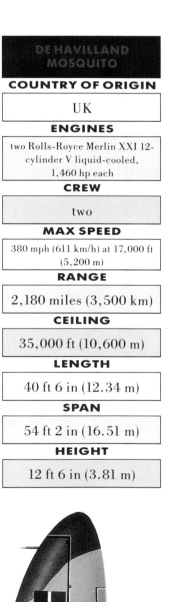

DE HAVILLAND MOSQUITO
COUNTRY OF ORIGIN
UK
ENGINES
two Rolls-Royce Merlin XXI 12-cylinder V liquid-cooled, 1,460 hp each
CREW
two
MAX SPEED
380 mph (611 km/h) at 17,000 ft (5,200 m)
RANGE
2,180 miles (3,500 km)
CEILING
35,000 ft (10,600 m)
LENGTH
40 ft 6 in (12.34 m)
SPAN
54 ft 2 in (16.51 m)
HEIGHT
12 ft 6 in (3.81 m)

Air observers had no trouble in recognizing the de Havilland Vampire, no matter how bad the weather, because of the distinctive whistling sound as it flew overhead. Any doubters should visit an airshow when the RAF 'Vintage Pair' display team, consisting of a Vampire and a Gloster Meteor, are performing.

Britain's second operational jet fighter, the Vampire made its first flight on 20 September 1943, although it did not enter service until May 1946. The prototype was given the unlikely name of 'Spider Crab' before the Vampire was adopted.

Although the Vampire was too late to see war service, it was a huge success, and over 4,000 were built and supplied to some 30 air forces around the world. The production total included numerous examples built under licence in Australia, France, India and Italy.

The original F.1 model was followed by many other variants culminating in the DH.115 Vampire T.11 side-by-side seat advanced trainer which equipped the RAF's flying schools until late 1967. Over 800 were built, as well as some 200 more under licence. On disposal, many RAF T.11s were allocated to Air Training Corps units but problems in maintaining the airframes meant that many wasted away.

The mark FB.52 was an export version of the FB.5 fighter bomber supplied to South Africa and many other countries. Numerous examples of the Vampire remain in South Africa including a FB.52 at the National Museum in Bloemfontein.

Above: The Vampire at the Royal Air Force Museum in Wales.

RAF ST. ATHAN HISTORIC AIRCRAFT COLLECTION

OWNER/OPERATOR	:	Royal Air Force Museum
ADDRESS	:	RAF St. Athan, Barry, South Glamorgan, Wales
LOCATION	:	About 12 miles (20 km) west of Cardiff. Road – B4265 to Cowbridge
ADMISSION	:	First Sunday in every month 1400-1700 otherwise prior permission only
FURTHER INFO	:	This outpost of the Royal Air Force Museum is due for closure, the aircraft eventually being moved to the museum's other collections.

DE HAVILLAND D.H.100 VAMPIRE

COUNTRY OF ORIGIN	UK
ENGINES	de Havilland Goblin 2 turbojet, 3,100 lb (1,420 kg) thrust
CREW	one
MAX SPEED	548 mph (882 km/h) at 30,000 ft (9,145 m)
RANGE	1,220 miles (1,960 km)
CEILING	44,000 ft (13,410 m)
LENGTH	30 ft 9 in (9.37 m)
SPAN	38 ft 0 in (11.58 m)
HEIGHT	8 ft 10 in (2.69 m)

The de Havilland Drover was designed and built at a time when Australia was trying to expand its own aircraft industry, the first prototype flying on 23 January 1948. Incorporating a number of structural features of the DH.104 Dove, the Drover was powered by three Gypsy Major 10 Mk 2 engines with manually-controlled variable pitch propellers. Limited production of the Drover was begun in 1949, but trouble with the vp propellers handicapped the first Drovers to enter service and these propellers were replaced by simple Fairey-Reed fixed pitch propellers. Machines modified in this way became known as the Drover 1F.

The first production Drover went into service as a freighter with Qantas Empire Airways in New Guinea, but it was in the Royal Flying Doctor Service, operated by Trans-Australian Airlines, that the Drovers found their true worth. Two stretcher cases were normally carried, together with medical attendants and equipment, and the Drover soon proved extremely popular. However, the aircraft was generally considered to be somewhat underpowered in order to climb to altitudes at which turbulence could be avoided, and seven Drovers were converted to take more powerful Lycoming engines. The first of the re-engined aircraft flew for the first time on 10 November, 1959 with the designation DHA.3. Twenty Drovers were built in all before production ended in 1953.

CENTRAL AUSTRALIAN AVIATION MUSEUM		
OWNER/OPERATOR	:	Central Australian Aviation Museum
ADDRESS	:	Memorial Avenue, Alice Springs, Northern Territory 5750
LOCATION	:	Half a mile west of the town centre
ADMISSION	:	Monday-Friday afternoons
FURTHER INFO	:	The museum is based in the one hangar and surrounding land that remains of the original Alice Springs Airport. It exists as a memorial to the pioneer aviators of Central Australia.

DE HAVILLAND D.H.A.3 DROVER 3
COUNTRY OF ORIGIN
Australia
ENGINES
three Lycoming O-360-A1A, 4-cylinder horizontally opposed, air-cooled, 180 hp each
CREW
two
MAX SPEED
144 mph (232 km/h)
RANGE
540 miles (870 km)
CEILING
not applicable
LENGTH
36 ft 2 in (11.02 m)
SPAN
57 ft 0 in (17.37 m)
HEIGHT
9 ft 9 in (2.97 m)

he Dornier Do.24 seaplane was originally designed to the requirements of the Royal Netherlands Naval Air Service for use in the East Indies. The prototype flew on 3 July 1937 and had a similar structural layout to that of the earlier Do.18, except that the Do.24 had three radial engines and twin fins and rudders. Deliveries of an initial batch of 12 aircraft – designated Do.24K – to the Dutch Government began in 1938, and licence production of a further 48 was undertaken by the Aviolanda and de Schelde factories in Holland. Twenty-five of these had been completed when the Germans overran the Netherlands in May 1940 and had gone to the Far East; some were lost in the fighting against the Japanese early in 1942, but a few escaped to Australia and were used by the Royal Australian Air Force for maritime patrol and air-sea rescue.

The unfinished Do.24s in Holland were shipped to Germany and completed there. They were operated by the Luftwaffe as Do.24N-1s in the air-sea rescue role. Production continued with the Do.24T-1 and Do.24T-2 reconnaissance and transport versions, of which 154 were built in Holland and 48 in occupied France. After the end of hostilities 22 of these aircraft were operated by the French Naval Air Arm. The Spanish Government purchased 12 Do.24Ts in 1944 and in 1953 bought a number of ex-French Navy machines, which were used in the search and rescue role until the late 1960s.

In the final days of the war in Europe it was a Do.24 that made the Luftwaffe's last flight into Berlin, landing on a lake under heavy fire and bringing out some senior German officers.

MUSEO DEL AIRE

OWNER/OPERATOR	:	Ejercito del Aire Espanol
ADDRESS	:	Cuatro Vientos, Madrid, Spain
LOCATION	:	About 6 miles (10 km) south west of Madrid. Road – NV
ADMISSION	:	Tuesday-Sunday 1000-1300
FURTHER INFO	:	The aircraft are displayed in a large exhibition hall and an adjacent landscaped park.

DORNIER Do.24

COUNTRY OF ORIGIN	
Germany	
ENGINES	
three BMW 323R-2 9-cylinder radial air-cooled, 1,000 hp each	
CREW	
four/five	
MAX SPEED	
206 mph (331 km/h) at 8,530 ft (2,600 m)	

RANGE
2,920 miles (4,700 km)
CEILING
24,605 ft (7,500 m)
LENGTH
72 ft 4 in (22.04 m)
SPAN
88 ft 7 in (27 m)
HEIGHT
18 ft 10 in (5.74 m)

In comparison with the vast number of Douglas DC-3/C-47/Dakota transports built, surprisingly only 370 Douglas B-18 Bolo bomber aircraft came off the production lines.

A little known type, with only a very few examples remaining, the Douglas B-18 was the bomber version of the company's highly successful DC series of commercial transports.

Initially a private venture by Douglas to meet a United States Army Air Corps requirement in 1934 for a modern twin engined bomber to replace the earlier Martin B-10B, the B-18 design incorporated much of the DC wing, engines and tail assembly to reduce costs and ease manufacture.

Two hundred and eight B-18 Bolos were built in two versions, the later being the B-18A which was introduced in 1937 and incorporated more powerful engines, a modified nose and a dorsal turret. Twenty of these were built for Canadian use.

Never a huge success, the B-18 managed to see service until the middle of World War II in the anti-submarine patrol role.

One of the few survivors, a 1937 vintage B-18A can be seen

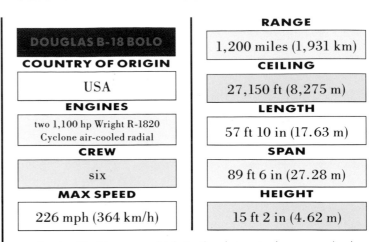

DOUGLAS B-18 BOLO	
COUNTRY OF ORIGIN	**RANGE**
USA	1,200 miles (1,931 km)
ENGINES	**CEILING**
two 1,100 hp Wright R-1820 Cyclone air-cooled radial	27,150 ft (8,275 m)
CREW	**LENGTH**
six	57 ft 10 in (17.63 m)
	SPAN
	89 ft 6 in (27.28 m)
MAX SPEED	**HEIGHT**
226 mph (364 km/h)	15 ft 2 in (4.62 m)

at Castle Air Museum which justly claims to have on display virtually all types of bomber used by the US Air Force and its predecessors from pre-World War II to the present day. The Bolo is the earliest type in the collection.

CASTLE AIR MUSEUM		
OWNER/OPERATOR	:	United States Air Force
ADDRESS	:	Castle Air Force Base, Atwater, California 95342
LOCATION	:	8 miles (13 km) north west of Merced. Road – off Highway 99
ADMISSION	:	Daily 1000-2000 (1600 in winter)
FURTHER INFO	:	This operational Strategic Air Command base is home to one of the largest air force base collections in the country.

he Douglas DC-1 was the precursor of the ubiquitous DC-3 Dakota, designed in response to the Boeing 247, the world's first modern airliner which featured an all-metal structure and retractable undercarriage. The Boeing design had been tailor-made for United Air Lines who subsequently purchased the full initial production capacity, effectively blocking out its competitors. Badly affected by the performance of United's new aircraft, which offered shorter flying time and a more comfortable and efficient service, TWA turned to Douglas in 1932 for an answer.

As history shows, the response was the DC-1, which led to the much improved DC-2 and then the DST (Douglas Sleeper Transport), especially designed for American Airlines, which evolved into the DC-3. In its civil and military version, known generally as the C-47, it became the best selling and most famous airliner ever, with almost 11,000 examples built.

The DC (Douglas Commercial) family of transports easily outperformed the Boeing 247, as illustrated during the Mac-Robertson England to Australia air race of 1934, when a KLM DC-2 finished second, ahead of its rival in third place.

The first DC-1 made its first flight on 1 July 1933 and TWA put the improved DC-2 into service on 18 May in the following year. A total of 198 DC-2s were built before production switched to the DST, American Airlines putting the first into service in May 1936. The first DC-3 soon followed. After service in the United States, it was sold to Brazil, where it still can be seen today in the VARIG Airlines museum.

THE PARACHUTE CENTRE

OWNER/OPERATOR	:	The Parachute Centre
ADDRESS	:	Lodi, California, USA
LOCATION	:	About 30 miles (48 km) south of Sacramento. Road – Route 99
ADMISSION	:	Free access
FURTHER INFO	:	The Parachute Centre operates a number of smartly turned out DC-3's.

DOUGLAS DC-3 DAKOTA

COUNTRY OF ORIGIN	**RANGE**
USA	1,510 miles (2,416 km)
ENGINES	**CEILING**
two Wright Cyclone SGR-1820-G2, 9-cylinder radial, air-cooled, 850-1,000 hp each	20,800 ft (6,340 m)
	LENGTH
	64 ft 5.5 in (19.65 m)
CREW	**SPAN**
two	95 ft 0 in (28.96 m)
MAX SPEED	**HEIGHT**
192 mph (309 km/h)	16 ft 3.6 in (4.97 m)

Left: The DC-3, used for promotional purposes at Bellingham Airfield in Washington State

Main picture: The DC-3 at the Parachute Centre, Lodi, California.

The mighty Douglas C-124 Globemaster II was the last USAF strategic transport aircraft to be powered by piston engines. Development began in 1947; the design was based on that of the earlier Douglas C-74 Globemaster, which had proved somewhat disappointing in service. Some C-74 components were used in the new aircraft, including the wings, engines and tailplane. The fuselage was completely designed and had two decks, the upper one accommodating up to 200 troops and the lower up to 31 tons of cargo. The aircraft had a large loading bay, with a built-in ramp under the nose.

The prototype Globemaster II flew on 27 December 1949. The aircraft was produced in two versions, the C-124A and the C-124C. The latter was fitted with more powerful Wasp Major engines. A total of 204 C-124As and 243 C-124Cs were built. The Globemaster II proved a valuable asset during the Korean War, two squadrons of the 374th Troop Carrier Wing beginning conversion to the type in May 1952. As the huge aircraft was designed to gross 175,000 lb (79,545 kg) on take-off, specially strengthened airstrips had to be laid at the key air bases in Korea so that it could operate without damaging the airfield surfaces. One vital task performed by the C-124 in Korea was to fly fuel tanks from the United States for the Fifth Air Force's F-86 Sabre jets, enabling them to maintain continual air superiority over the Yalu River.

In the late 1950s, C-124s were used extensively to ferry nuclear weapons components to Strategic Air Command bases worldwide. The aircraft remained in USAF service until 1961.

KOREAN WAR MUSEUM		
OWNER/OPERATOR	:	United Nations War Allies Association
ADDRESS	:	May 16 Plaza, Yoi-Do, Seoul-Cpo box 936, South Korea
LOCATION	:	on Yeo-ení island in the city centre
ADMISSION	:	Daily 0900-1700
FURTHER INFO	:	Surrounded by high-rise buildings, the museum commemorates the 1950-53 Korean War. In addition to some 12 aircraft, it has on display a number of army fighting vehicles, arms, uniforms and many other items.

DOUGLAS C-124C GLOBEMASTER II	
COUNTRY OF ORIGIN	
USA	
ENGINES	
four Pratt & Whitney R-4360-63A Wasp Majors 28/cylinder air-cooled radials, 3,800 hp each	
CREW	
eight	
MAX SPEED	
230 mph (370 km/h)	
RANGE	
4,030 miles (6,480 km)	
CEILING	
18,400 ft (5,600 m)	
LENGTH	
130 ft 0 in (39.62 m)	
SPAN	
174 ft 2 in (53.08 m)	
HEIGHT	
48 ft 4 in (14.73 m)	

The Douglas C-118 was the military transport version of the DC-6 civil airliner, which in turn was developed from the DC-4 (C-54) Skymaster. The C-118 was basically a DC-6A, incorporating a cargo loading door and a strengthened fuselage floor. The aircraft was also supplied to the United States Navy as the R6D Liftmaster; 167 were built in total. The C-118/R6D could accommodate 76 troops, 40 stretchers or 25,000 lb (11,363 kg) of cargo in addition to a normal crew of five. A few were converted to VIP standard under the designation VC-118.

The C-118 performed excellent service with the US Military Air Transport Service during the 1950s and 1960s, and were used mainly by the 29th, 30th and 38th Air Transport Squadrons of the 1611th Air Transport Wing at McGuire Air Force Base, New Jersey. The aircraft were used regularly on the transatlantic routes in support of the United States Air Forces in Europe.

Some C-118s were converted for photo survey work under the designation RC-118; these were used by the 1370th Photo Mapping Wing at Turner Air Force Base, Georgia, and operated on tasks set by the US Air Photographic and Charting Service. This work extended to all spheres of USAF activity around the world. C-118s were also operated by the 1298th Air Transport Squadron at Andrews Air Force Base, Maryland, and the 48th Air Transport Squadron at Hickam Air Force Base, Hawaii.

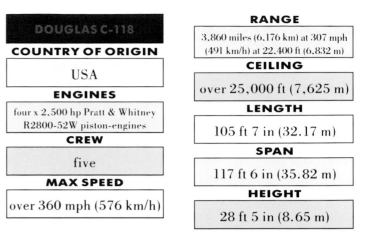

DOUGLAS C-118	
COUNTRY OF ORIGIN	
USA	
ENGINES	
four x 2,500 hp Pratt & Whitney R2800-52W piston-engines	
CREW	
five	
MAX SPEED	
over 360 mph (576 km/h)	

RANGE
3,860 miles (6,176 km) at 307 mph (491 km/h) at 22,400 ft (6,832 m)
CEILING
over 25,000 ft (7,625 m)
LENGTH
105 ft 7 in (32.17 m)
SPAN
117 ft 6 in (35.82 m)
HEIGHT
28 ft 5 in (8.65 m)

PIMA AIR MUSEUM

OWNER/OPERATOR	:	United States Air Force
ADDRESS	:	6400 South Wilmot Road, Tucson, Arizona 85706, USA
LOCATION	:	About 12 miles (20 km) south east of Tucson. Road – Interstate 10
ADMISSION	:	Daily 0900-1700
FURTHER INFO	:	The museum is situated nearby the Davis-Monthan AFB which is the major aircraft storage and disposal facility for the United States Air Force.

Above: The Douglas C-118 in another guise: for civilian use as the DC-6.

Below: Travis Air Force Base, in California, exhibits the C–118.

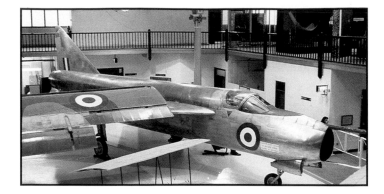

he first and only purely British-designed and built supersonic fighter for the Royal Air Force was the distinctive English Electric (later British Aircraft Corporation) Lightning. Unique in its configuration, the design originated in the P.1A and P.1B experimental aircraft which thrilled the crowds in the late 1950s at the Farnborough Air Show – the shop window of Britain's aircraft industry.

The first P.1A prototype made its maiden flight in the hands of test pilot Roland Beamont on 4 August 1954, with the second taking to the air on 18 July 1955. Two P.1Bs and three Lightning prototypes followed, together with 20 pre-production machines before series production began.

The Lightning entered service with the Royal Air Force in 1960, with No 74 (Tiger) Squadron. Part of their duties was to act as the official RAF air display team, superseding the famous Black Arrows, 111 Squadron with their Hawker Hunter aircraft.

Following withdrawal from service in 1988, the Ministry of Defence put their remaining Lightnings up for sale at knock-down prices. As a result, many examples have ended their days in aircraft collections, with at least one group attempting to put a T.4 trainer variant back into flying condition.

The second prototype P.1A, WG763, survives as an exhibit at the Museum of Science and Industry in Manchester, which contains an excellent Aviation Gallery. The location is fitting since the P.1 and the subsequent Lightning were designed and built in English Electric's factories in the same region.

MUSEUM OF SCIENCE AND INDUSTRY AVIATION GALLERY		
OWNER/OPERATOR	:	Museum of Science and Industry
ADDRESS	:	Liverpool Road, Castlefield, Manchester M3 4JP
LOCATION	:	Manchester City Centre
ADMISSION	:	Every day 1030-1700
FURTHER INFO	:	The museum has been created around the world's first passenger railway station.

Top right: The P.1A, the prototype for the Lightning, at the Museum of Science and Industry in Manchester.

Inset: The Lightning T-4.

Below: The Lightning F.1A, at Leuchars Air Force Base in Scotland.

ENGLISH ELECTRIC P.1A		RANGE
COUNTRY OF ORIGIN		n/a
UK		**CEILING**
ENGINES		50,000 ft 0 in (15,500 m)
two 10,200 lb s t (4,630 kg s t) Bristol Siddeley Sapphire turbojets		**LENGTH**
		50 ft 0 in (15.5 m)
CREW		**SPAN**
one		34 ft 10 in (10.82 m)
MAX SPEED		**HEIGHT**
1,520 mph (2,447 km/h) or Mach 2.3 at altitude		19 ft 7 in (6.06 m)

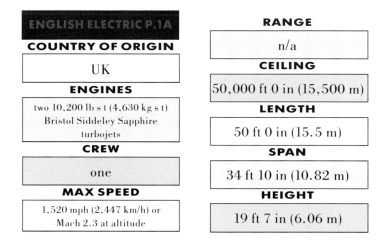

he Fairchild C-119 was a modified version of the Fairchild Corporation's first post-war transport design, the C-82A Packet. Some 220 were delivered to the USAF between the end of 1945 and 1948, when production ceased. In the meantime, the C-119 had made its first flight in November 1947, with deliveries beginning in December 1949. The first production batch of 55 aircraft, designated C-119Bs, was followed by 347 C-119Cs with more powerful engines and slight structural modifications. The next version was the C-119F, which was fitted with Wright R-3350 engines developing 3,500 hp at take-off and driving four-bladed propellers; these made it possible to increase the take-off weight to over 38 tons. A total of 216 C-119Fs were built before production gave way to the last of the series, the C-119G, which differed from its predecessor only in the type of propeller fitted.

The C-119 saw extensive service in the Korean War, in which it carried out some noteworthy operations. In December 1950, for example, with the Allied forces in retreat before a massive Chinese onslaught, they air-dropped several bridge spans to the 1st US Marine Division, which had become trapped when the enemy destroyed vital bridges in the Koto-Ri sector. The bridge spans were quickly put in place and the Marines escaped with their vehicles and equipment.

C-119 production ended in October 1955, by which time 1,112 had been built. As well as seeing widespread service with the USAF and the US Navy (as the R4Q), the C-119 also served with the air forces of Belgium, Brazil, Canada, Nationalist China, India, Italy, Morocco and Norway. Some USAF C-119s were specially modified for reconnaissance satellite recovery.

CALIFORNIAN DEPARTMENT OF FORESTRY	
OWNER/OPERATOR :	Helmet Valley Air Service of California
ADDRESS :	Paso Robles, California, USA
LOCATION :	About 30 miles (48 km) north of San Lois Obispo. Road – Route 466
ADMISSION :	Free access
FURTHER INFO :	Designated an 'air attack station', Lodi is also the maintenance base and winter overall facility for the Californian Department of Forestry.

Above: The Flying Boxcar at Paso Robles in California.
Below: At the Pima Air Museum in Arizona.

FAIRCHILD C-119 FLYING BOXCAR	
COUNTRY OF ORIGIN	
USA	
ENGINES	
two Wright R-3350-89 Cyclones 18-cylinder air-cooled radials, 3,500 hp each	
CREW	
four	
MAX SPEED	
218 mph (350 km/h) at 10,000 ft (3,050 m)	
RANGE	
1,770 miles (2,850 km)	
CEILING	
23,900 ft (7,285 m)	
LENGTH	
86 ft 6 in (26.36 m)	
SPAN	
109 ft 4 in (33.32 m)	
HEIGHT	
26 ft 3 in (8 m)	

The Fairey Firefly was a wartime design which entered service with the Fleet Air Arm in 1943. It saw much operational service before the end of hostilities, including attacks on the German battleship *Tirpitz*, a strike on the Japanese-held oil refineries in Sumatra and missions over the Japanese home islands while operating with Task Force 57 in the Pacific. The Firefly also equipped eight FAA squadrons at the end of World War II. Most of these were subsequently disbanded, but from October 1945, 11 other FAA units re-equipped with the type. These were mostly the Firefly FR.4 or FR.5, but one — 827 Squadron — was still using the earlier FR.1 in 1949, and in December that year it began a series of strikes against terrorist hideouts in Malaya, flying from the light fleet carrier HMS *Triumph*. 827 Squadron was also the first Firefly squadron to see action in Korea, on 30 June 1950. The Firefly continued to operate with considerable success throughout the Korean War, serving with 810 Squadron (HMS *Theseus*), 812 and 820 (HMS *Glory*), 817 (HMAS *Sydney*) and 825 (HMS *Ocean*).

The Firefly AS.6 was a three-seat anti-submarine variant which entered service in 1951 and equipped five Fleet Air Arm squadrons, as well as six squadrons of the Royal Naval Volunteer Reserve. In 1954, the Firefly AS.6s of 825 Squadron carried out a series of ground attack missions against terrorists in Malaya, the last occasion the type fired its guns in anger.

Total production of the Firefly (all marks, up to the U Mk 8 target drone) was 1,702 aircraft, and the type was supplied to Australia, Canada, Denmark, Ethiopia, India, the Netherlands, Sweden and Thailand. The Dutch aircraft — FR.1s — saw action against rebel forces in the Dutch East Indies.

WAR MEMORIAL		
ADDRESS	:	Griffith, New South Wales, Australia
LOCATION	:	In the town centre
ADMISSION	:	Free access
FURTHER INFO	:	The Royal Australian Navy operated the Fairey Firefly from August 1948–March 1966.

FAIREY FIREFLY		RANGE
COUNTRY OF ORIGIN		1,300 miles (2,100 km)
UK		**CEILING**
ENGINES		28,000 ft (8,500 m)
Rolls-Royce Griffon 11B 12-cylinder V liquid-cooled, 1,730 hp		**LENGTH**
		37 ft 7 in (11.46 m)
CREW		**SPAN**
two		44 ft 6 in (13.56 m)
MAX SPEED		**HEIGHT**
316 mph (508 km/h) at 14,000 ft (4,250 m)		13 ft 7 in (4.14 m)

An indigenous design built by Argentina's Fabrica Militar de Aviones (FMA), the Pucara was produced in response for a light attack aircraft for the air force.

For use in both the counter-insurgency and close-support roles, design started in 1966 and the first prototype made its first flight on 20 August, 1969. Production did not commence until 1974 and the initial orders for 45 aircraft began reaching operational units in 1976.

A sleek twin-turboprop powered aircraft with a good all-round performance, the Pucara was, however, an unsophisticated design. Heavily used in the Falklands conflict of 1982, some 24 were lost to British attacks. To improve the aircraft's capabilities, a revised version known as the IA-58C Pucara Charlie was flown in 1985. A single-seater, it featured improved avionics and equipment and carried a greater range of armaments.

Following the conflict, several examples were taken to the UK for evaluation and museum display. One example remained at RAF Stanley airfield where, under the direction of Mark

FALKLAND ISLANDS MUSEUM	
ADDRESS	: Port Stanley, Falkland Islands
LOCATION	: One for display at Port Stanley
ADMISSION	: Not available
FURTHER INFO	: The Pucara and a Bell UH-1H Huey are being stored at RAF Mount Pleasant awaiting completion of the museum.

Harrisson, it was rebuilt by volunteers from both the Army and RAF.

Registered A-529, the Pucara received parts from sister ships A-514 and A-509 while other items, such as the propellers and canopy perspex were made locally. During the restoration work, the aircraft was completely stripped down, protected and rebuilt.

Above and right: The Falkland Island Museum, and the Aerospace Museum in Shropshire both exhibit examples of the Pucara.

FMA IA-58 PUCARA	
COUNTRY OF ORIGIN	**RANGE**
	1,890 miles (3,042 km)
Argentina	**CEILING**
	32,810 ft (10,000 m)
ENGINES	**LENGTH**
two Turbomeca Astazou XVIG turboprops, 1,022 hp each	46 ft 9 in (14.25 m)
CREW	**SPAN**
two	47 ft 7 in (14.50 m)
MAX SPEED	**HEIGHT**
310 mph (500 km/h)	17 ft 7 in (5.36 m)

A creation of the famous German designer Kurt Tank, the Stieglitz was one of the standard primary trainers used in Germany's pre-war military flying training programme, and large quantities were supplied to the Luftwaffe. As well as being exported to Bolivia, Bulgaria, Chile, China, Finland, Hungary, Rumania, Sweden, Turkey and Slovakia, the aircraft was built under licence in Argentina, Brazil, Turkey and Sweden. Argentina was still using its Fw44s as late as 1960.

An attractive two-seat biplane with wooden wings, a fuselage of fabric-covered welded steel tube, and a split-axle undercarriage with faired main legs, the Stieglitz first flew in the late summer of 1932, and was initially powered by the 150 hp Siemens Sh14a radial engine. A few examples of the Fw44C, with the 135 hp Argus As8 in-line engine, were built, and then followed the slightly modified Fw44D (Sh14a) and Fw44E (As8), the radial-engined version being produced in far greater numbers. The export variant was the Fw44J. In 1944 no fewer than 700 Stieglitz were in service with the Luftwaffe.

The Stieglitz was also popular with private owners, and one was owned by the World War I ace Ernst Udet, who used it for sporting and aerobatic flying. Another celebrated German pilot, Gerd Achgelis, flew an Fw44 in the 1934 US National Air Races at Cleveland, Ohio, and in the 1934 World Aerobatic Championships at Vincennes, France. Many are maintained in flying condition throughout Germany and Scandinavia, the example depicted here being kept at Fassberg, in Germany.

FASSBERG	
OWNER/OPERATOR :	H T Pfeiffer
LOCATION :	25 miles (40 km) north of Celle
ADMISSION :	Prior permission only
FURTHER INFO :	The Luftwaffe Technical Training Unit, Apprentice School and Fire Training School have between them a large collection of past and present military types.

FOCKE-WULF Fw44 STIEGLITZ	
COUNTRY OF ORIGIN	
Germany	
ENGINES	
one 150 hp Siemens SH14A radial	
CREW	
two	
MAX SPEED	
155 mph (248 km)	
RANGE	
420 miles (672 km)	
CEILING	
12,800 ft (3,902 m)	
LENGTH	
23 ft 11 in (7.30 m)	
SPAN	
29 ft 6 in (9.0 m)	
HEIGHT	
8 ft 10 in (2.78 m)	

Originally designed as a result of a German air ministry suggestion that Focke-Wulfe should develop a fighter to be built concurrently with the Messerschmitt Bf 109, the Fw 190 became Germany's best fighter of World War II.

Designer Kurt Tank produced two proposals and, despite some misgivings, the version chosen was powered by an air-cooled radial engine. Three prototypes were constructed, the first flying on 1 June 1939. Despite early problems with overheating, initial trials went very well for Germany's first radial-engined monoplane fighter.

The Fw 190 went into service during July 1941 and immediately proved itself to be faster and more manoeuvrable than the Spitfire V. Numerous developments followed as 13,367 machines were produced in ten versions as interceptors while a further 6,634 were built in two versions as fighter-bombers.

The ultimate fighter version was the Fw 190D which was powered by a Junkers Jumo liquid-cooled inline engine which, with power boost, gave a maximum speed of 453 mph (729 km/h) at 37,000 ft (11,470 m). With the increased performance the D model was a match for the North American P-51D Mustang.

Five Fw 190Ds were brought to the United States for evaluation after the war and one survived with the Georgia Technical University. Having been purchased by Doug Champlin for his Fighter Museum in Mesa, Arizona in 1972, the aircraft was returned to Germany for restoration by Arthur Williams, helped by no other than Kurt Tank himself.

The aircraft returned to the United States in 1976, where it takes pride of place in the Champlin Fighter Museum.

CHAMPLIN FIGHTER MUSEUM

OWNER/OPERATOR :	Doug Champlin
ADDRESS :	4636 Fighter Aces Drive, Mesa, Arizona 85205
LOCATION :	Falcon Field Airport, 3 miles north of Mesa
ADMISSION :	Daily 1000-1700 (except public holidays)
FURTHER INFO :	The museum is the home of the American Fighter Aces Association who have a large collection of memorabilia on display.

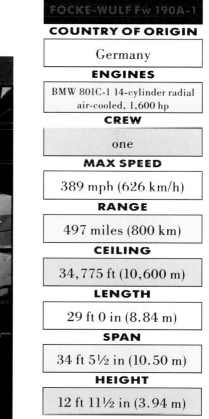

FOCKE-WULF Fw 190A-1

COUNTRY OF ORIGIN
Germany
ENGINES
BMW 801C-1 14-cylinder radial air-cooled, 1,600 hp
CREW
one
MAX SPEED
389 mph (626 km/h)
RANGE
497 miles (800 km)
CEILING
34,775 ft (10,600 m)
LENGTH
29 ft 0 in (8.84 m)
SPAN
34 ft 5½ in (10.50 m)
HEIGHT
12 ft 11½ in (3.94 m)

Top: The Focke Wulf in the collection of Doug Champlin.
Above: The model at the National Air and Space Museum, Silver Hill, Maryland.

Considered one of the most important American transport aircraft ever designed as it became the mainstay of many of the country's first major airlines, the Fort 4-AT was, in fact, based on the highly successful Dutch Fokker FVII/3m.

Henry Ford had acquired an example from Anthony Fokker as he was to act as sales agent in the United States. However, his chief engineer saw the development potential and the 4-AT Tri-Motor evolved using Junker's patented method of all-metal construction, as used on the Ju 52/3m 'Tante Ju'.

The original 4-AT first flew in 1926 and could carry 11 passengers, powered by either 235 hp or 300 hp Wright Whirlwind engines. The 5-AT was launched two years later, with an enlarged wing, seating for two more passengers and powered by three 450 hp Whirlwinds or 420 hp Pratt & Whitney Wasps.

Acknowledging the basic integrity and efficiency of the original design, an updated version known as the Bushmaster 200 was designed and built in 1966, although production never took place.

Earlier confirmation of the sturdiness and reliability of Fokker's concept were shown by Lt Cdr Richard Byrd, USN, who flew to the North Pole in a Fokker F.VII/3m in 1927 and then to the South Pole in a Ford Tri-Motor in 1934, being the first man to fly over both Poles.

A number of Ford Tri-Motors still exist, including several in flying condition which are used for scenic pleasure flights.

Right: The Ford Tri-motor on exhibition at the Henley Aerodrome and (below) at the Henry Ford Museum in Dearborn, Michigan.

HENLEY AERODROME AND MUSEUM OF TRANSPORTATION	
OWNER/OPERATOR :	Gary and Stacey Norton
ADDRESS :	Route 1, Box 98V, Athol, Idaho 83801
LOCATION :	3 miles south of Athol. Road – Route 95
ADMISSION :	Daily 0900-1700
FURTHER INFO :	Complementing the aircraft collection is a display of historic vehicles. A scenic railway has been constructed round the airfield with a train hauled by a 1915 Porter steam engine.

FORD 4-AT TRI-MOTOR	
COUNTRY OF ORIGIN	
USA	
ENGINES	
Three Wright J6 Whirlwind, 9-cylinder radial, air-cooled 200 hp each	
CREW	
two	
MAX SPEED	
107 mph (172 km/h)	
RANGE	
570 miles (920 km)	
CEILING	
16,400 ft (5,000 m)	
LENGTH	
49 ft 10 in (15.19 m)	
SPAN	
74 ft 0 in (22.56 m)	
HEIGHT	
11 ft 9 in (3.58 m)	

asily recognizable by its butterfly tail, the Fouga C.M. 170 Magister was one of the most successful jet trainers of the 1950s, operated by air forces around the world from Guatemala to Bangladesh.

Initially designed as a twin-seat turbojet powered *ab initio* for the French Air Force, the Magister made its first flight on 23 July 1952. An order for 400 machines from L'Armée de l'Air was the start of a flood of interest from many other countries.

The Luftwaffe ordered 250 examples, of which 188 were built under licence. The Magister was also licence built in Finland and Israel where Israel Aircraft Industries greatly modified the type as the IAI Improved Magister. As well as retaining these modified aircraft for their own use, Israel supplied a number to El Salvador.

A naval variant with more powerful engines and deck landing capability, the C.M. 175 Zephyr, was developed for the French Navy who ordered 45 aircraft. The prototype made its maiden flight on 31 July 1956. The final French version was the Super Magister, which first appeared in 1962. In line with developments at the time, the Magister was developed as an armed ground support and counter insurgency (COIN) aircraft, equipped with two machine guns and able to carry both rockets and bombs.

An early Magister, the fifth pre-production machine, can be seen in what is probably the nicest location for an aircraft museum – a vineyard. The Musée d'Avions au Mas Palegry was founded by former air force pilot Charles Noetinger at his vineyard where he has a number of aircraft on display.

MUSEE D'AVIONS AU MAS PALEGRY	
OWNER/OPERATOR :	Charles Noetinger
ADDRESS :	Chemin de Villeneuve de la Raho, Mas Palegry, Perpignon 6000, France
LOCATION :	4 km south of Perpignon. Road – between RN9 and RN114
ADMISSION :	July and August – afternoons
FURTHER INFO :	A small, private museum situated in M. Noetinger's estate, the aircraft are as interesting as his wines.

POTEZ-AIR FOUGA C.M. 170 MAGISTER

COUNTRY OF ORIGIN	
France	
ENGINES	
two Turbomeca Marbore II turbojets each rated at 836 lb s t	
CREW	
two	
MAX SPEED	
402 mph (643 km/h) at sea level, 443 mph (708 km/h) at 30,000 ft (9,146 m)	

RANGE	
576 miles (921 km) at 30,000 ft	
CEILING	
44,500 ft (13,567 m)	
LENGTH	
33 ft 0 in (10.06 m)	
SPAN	
37 ft 1 in (11.30 m)	
HEIGHT	
9 ft 2 in (2.80 m)	

A rguably the most successful of the first generation jet fighters, the Gloster Meteor was the only Allied jet aircraft to see service during World War II.

The initial order for eight prototypes and 20 production F.1s was placed in September 1941. While the first prototype was completed in mid-1942 and taxying trials took place immediately, the first flight of the type did not occur until 5 March 1943 because of a lack of engines that could produce sufficient power.

The first squadron to fly the Meteor operationally during the war was No 616, who received their first aircraft on 12 July 1944. The aircraft was to stay in front-line service with the Royal Air Force in various marks until July 1961, by which time 3,850 had been built in the UK and the Netherlands under licence and supplied to some 12 air forces worldwide.

Following the end of hostilities, several Meteor F.4s were transferred to the RAF's High Speed Flight. In modified form, they were used to raise the world air speed record to 606 mph (976 km/h) on 7 November 1945, and then 616 mph (992 km/h) the following 7 September, the aircraft being flown by Gp Capt E M Donaldson.

Initially named the Rampage or Thunderbolt (the latter name was dropped because of confusion with the Republic design of the same name), the Meteor nearly gathered yet another name tag. Designed and funded as a private venture, the Gloster G44 ground attack development of the Meteor incorporated a strengthened F.4 wing and F.8 rear fuselage. Named the Reaper, it first flew in 1951, but with the company lacking any orders, the sole example was de-militarized in 1954 and converted to a T.7, ending its days with Svedino's Bil Och Flygmuseum in Sweden.

SVEDINO'S BIL OCH FLYGMUSEUM	
OWNER/OPERATOR :	Lennart Svedfelt
ADDRESS :	Vgglarp, Sloinge 531050, Sweden
LOCATION :	Approx. 25 km northwest of Halmstad on the coast road to Falkenberg
ADMISSION :	April–October (except July, August) Saturday-Sunday 1000-1700. July-August daily 1000-1700
FURTHER INFO :	Many ex-Swedish air force types share this privately run museum with a number of civil light aircraft and over 120 cars.

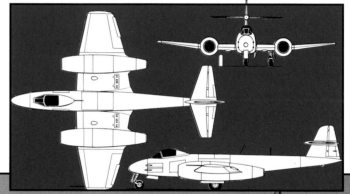

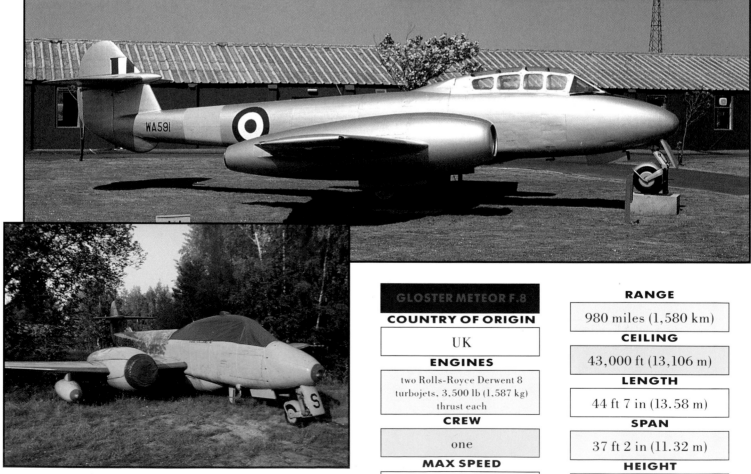

Main picture: The Gloster Meteor F8 at RAF Woodvale.
Inset: The Reaper at the Flygmuseum in Sweden.

GLOSTER METEOR F.8		RANGE
COUNTRY OF ORIGIN		980 miles (1,580 km)
UK		**CEILING**
ENGINES		43,000 ft (13,106 m)
two Rolls-Royce Derwent 8 turbojets, 3,500 lb (1,587 kg) thrust each		**LENGTH**
		44 ft 7 in (13.58 m)
CREW		**SPAN**
one		37 ft 2 in (11.32 m)
MAX SPEED		**HEIGHT**
598 mph (962 km/h) at 33,000 ft (10,000 m)		13 ft 0 in (3.96 m)

The Grumman J2/J2F series of amphibious biplanes served as utility transport and liaison aircraft with the US Navy from 1934 and the US Coast Guard from 1935 until well after the end of World War II, a record of reliability and ruggedness hardly matched by any other type designed during the inter-war years. The prototype flew in 1933 and initial production JF-1s were powered by Pratt & Whitney Twin Wasp engines, although this was changed to a Wright Cyclone for the later JF-2, the Coast Guard version, and the JF-3. On 20 November 1934 a JF-2 flown by E F Stone established a speed record for this class of aircraft of 191.734 mph.

The name 'Duck' was adopted by the US Navy and covered the J2F-1 to J2F-6, which were fitted with deck arrester gear and catapult points in the central float for aircraft carrier operations. Total production was 55 JFs and 560 J2Fs, with most of the latter built from 1941 onwards. In 1970, a J2F-6 Duck brought to an airworthy condition by Frank Tallman was used in the making of the film *Murphy's War*, for which it was painted in spurious Royal Navy markings.

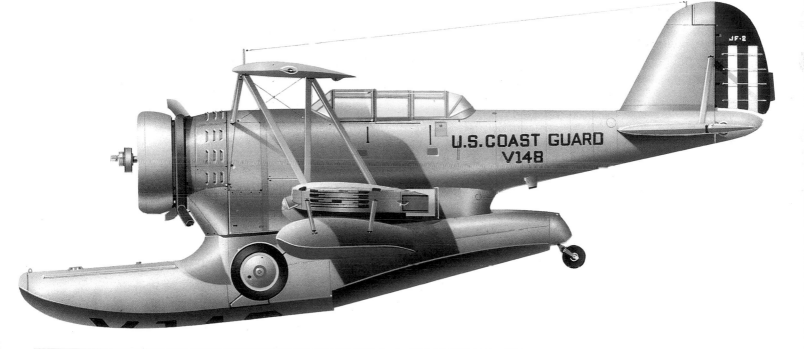

WEEKS AIR MUSEUM	
OWNER/OPERATOR :	Kermit Weeks
ADDRESS :	14710 Southwest 128th St, Miami, Florida
LOCATION :	Tamiami Airport. In south west suburbs of the city
ADMISSION :	Saturday-Sunday 1000-1700
FURTHER INFO :	Aerobatic pilot Kermit Weeks has built up one of the most significant aircraft collections in the United States.

GRUMMAN J2F-5 DUCK
COUNTRY OF ORIGIN
USA
ENGINES
Wright R-1820-50 Cyclone 9-cylinder radial, air-cooled, 850 hp
CREW
two
MAX SPEED
188 mph (302 km/h)

RANGE	
780 miles (1,255 km)	
CEILING	
27,000 ft (8,230 m)	
LENGTH	
34 ft 0 in (10.36 m)	
SPAN	
39 ft 0 in (11.89 m)	
HEIGHT	
15 ft 1 in (4.60 m)	

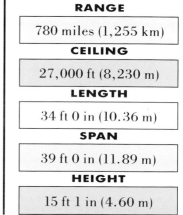

The Grumman TBF Avenger torpedo-bomber was designed to replace the Douglas Devastator, which suffered heavy losses during anti-shipping attacks in the early stages of the Pacific War. Two XTBF-1 prototypes were ordered by the US Navy in April 1940, and a substantial production order had been placed by the time the first of these flew on 1 August 1941. The first production TBF-1s went into service with Squadron VT-8 in January 1942. Its combat debut was inauspicious — five out of six aircraft were shot down by Japanese Zero fighters during an heroic but unsuccessful attack by VT-8 on enemy warships during the Battle of Midway — but it went on to become one of the most celebrated naval attack aircraft ever, widely used in the Atlantic as well as the Pacific.

Up to December 1943 Grumman built 2,293 Avengers, of which 402 were supplied to the Royal Navy and 63 to the Royal New Zealand Air Force. Avenger production was also undertaken by the Eastern Aircraft Division of General Motors, which built 2,882 as the TBM-1 and TBM-1C. Of these, 334 went to the Royal Navy as Avenger IIs. Eastern went on to complete 4,665 TBM-3s, with wings strengthened to carry rocket projectiles or a radar pod; 222 of these became the Royal Navy's Avenger III. Because of some difficulty in installing British torpedos in the American aircraft, the RN Avengers were used as bombers, minelayers or rocket-firing strike aircraft. Until January 1944, when the name Avenger was standardized, the British aircraft were known as Tarpons.

American and British Avengers played an important role in the final assault on Japan, and the type remained in service for many years after the war.

MUSEUM OF TRANSPORT & TECHNOLOGY		
ADDRESS	:	Great North Road, Western Springs, Auckland 2, New Zealand
LOCATION	:	2 miles southwest of the city centre
ADMISSION	:	Daily 0900-1700
FURTHER INFO	:	The museum represents all types of transport and holds regular 'live' weekends. The main site is connected by a tramway to a 20-acre park where the larger aircraft are exhibited.

Below: The Museum of Transport and Technology, Auckland, includes the Avenger in its collection.

Above: The example on display at the Canadian Warplane Heritage, Ontario.

GRUMMAN TBF-1 AVENGER
COUNTRY OF ORIGIN
USA
ENGINES
Wright R-2600-8 Cyclone 14-cylinder radial air-cooled, 1,700 hp
CREW
three
MAX SPEED
271 mph (436 km/h) at 12,000 ft (3,660 m)
RANGE
1,215 miles (1,950 km)
CEILING
22,400 ft (6,800 m)
LENGTH
40 ft 0 in (12.19 m)
SPAN
54 ft 2 in (16.51 m)
HEIGHT
16 ft 5 in (5 m)

O ne of the most important carrier-borne anti-submarine aircraft of the post-war years, the proto-type Grumman XS2F-1 Tracker flew for the first time on 4 December 1952. First deliveries were made to Navy Squadron VS-26 in February 1954, and at the end of that year the type embarked on the USS *Princeton* with VS-23. A total of 755 examples of the initial production series of S2F-1s were built, and the type was also supplied to Argentina, Japan, Italy, Brazil, Taiwan, Thailand, Uruguay and the Netherlands.

The S-2C, which was next on the assembly line, featured a larger torpedo bay capable of housing homing torpedos. Sixty were built, and most of these were later converted to US-2C cargo aircraft. The S-2D was a developed version with an in-creased wingspan and improved crew accommodation, as well as more advanced weaponry and avionics. It had twice the endurance of the S2F-1 (or S-2A, as it was later redesignated) when giving 'round the fleet' anti-submarine coverage at a radius of 230 miles. The S-2E was an upgraded version with still more advanced equipment, and could carry 5-inch rockets on underwing racks.

The S-2A Tracker was built under licence in Canada by de Havilland Aircraft Ltd, the Canadian version being designated CS2F-1. Further variants were the CS2F-2 and CS2F-3. The first two versions were operated from shore bases, while the CS2F-3 was used by Squadron VS-880 aboard the carrier HMCS *Bonaventure*. Of the 100 CS2F-1 Trackers built in Canada, 17 were supplied to the Royal Netherlands Navy and 12 to the Brazilian Navy, the latter batch operating from the carrier *Minas Gerais*. Variants of the basic Tracker design were the C-1A Trader general purpose aircraft and the E-1B Tracer, which was modified for early warning and fighter direction.

INTREPID AIR-SEA-SPACE MUSEUM

OWNER/OPERATOR	:	Intrepid Foundation
ADDRESS	:	Intrepid Square, West 46th Street and 12th Avenue, New York 10036
LOCATION	:	Pier 86 on the west side of Manhattan Island
ADMISSION	:	Wednesday-Sunday 1000-1700
FURTHER INFO	:	The aircraft are aboard *USS Intrepid*, an aircraft carrier launched in 1943 and served with distinction before becoming a floating city-centre museum in 1980.

Top: The Grumman S2-E Tracker at the Intrepid Air-Sea-Space Museum, New York.

Bottom: The Grumman C-1 Trader, photographed at Pensacola, Florida.

GRUMMAN S-2A TRACKER

COUNTRY OF ORIGIN
USA

ENGINES
two Wright R-1820-82 WA Cyclone 9-cylinder air-cooled radials, 1,525 hp each

CREW
four

MAX SPEED
287 mph (461 km/h) at 5,000 ft (1,524 m)

RANGE
900 miles (1,450 km)

CEILING
23,000 ft (7,010 m)

LENGTH
42 ft 3 in (12.87 m)

SPAN
69 ft 8 in (21.23 m)

HEIGHT
16 ft 3 in (4.95 m)

t is said that if an aircraft looks right, then it is right. If this is so, one such aircraft was the Handley Page Hastings, designed as a heavy freighter and troop transport during the closing stages of World War II. Entering service in October 1948, the Hastings immediately saw operational service in the Berlin Airlift where it earned its reputation as a workhorse.

An initial batch of 100 C.Mk.1s was built for RAF Transport Command squadrons, followed up by a further 50 improved C.Mk.2s which had a greater all-up weight and payload together with a longer range. In addition to service with the RAF in both the Near and Far East as well as Europe and the UK, four Hastings were supplied to the Royal New Zealand Air Force as the C.Mk.3. Variants included the Hastings Met.Mk.1 for long range meteorological reconnaissance, and the C.Mk.4 VIP version.

The then British sector airfield for the Berlin Airlift was Gatow and preserved there in memoriam is Hastings TG503, the fifth production C.Mk.1, together with a Royal Australian Air Force Dakota. Both machines are actually owned by Berlin's Transport and Technology Museum.

Completing the round-up, Berlin's French sector airfield of Tegel has preserved a Nord Noratlas while the old American sector airfield of Templehof displays a Douglas C-54 Skymaster and a Douglas C-47 Dakota.

RAF GATOW	
OWNER/OPERATOR :	Museum Fur Verkehr Und Technik
ADDRESS :	RAF Gatow, West Berlin, Germany
LOCATION :	In the original British sector of West Berlin
ADMISSION :	Free access
FURTHER INFO :	The Hastings and an ex-Royal Australian Air Force Dakota are preserved as a memorial to the Berlin Airlift.

Below: The Hastings TG503 seen in its final operational colour scheme at RAF Gutersloh, Berlin, and *right*, as it appears today at Gatow.

HANDLEY PAGE HASTINGS C.1	
COUNTRY OF ORIGIN	
UK	
ENGINES	
four Bristol Hercules 106 14-cylinder air-cooled radials, 1,675 hp each	
CREW	
five	
MAX SPEED	
348 mph (560 km/h) at 22,200 ft (6,770 m)	
RANGE	
4,250 miles (6,840 km)	
CEILING	
26,500 ft (8,080 m)	
LENGTH	
82 ft 8 in (25.19 m)	
SPAN	
113 ft 0 in (34.44 m)	
HEIGHT	
22 ft 6 in (6.85 m)	

Although the Spitfire took the glory for the RAF's success during the Battle of Britain, the brunt of the fighting was borne by the Hawker Hurricane. Less agile and with a lower performance, the Hurricane was nevertheless a very rugged aircraft which could absorb a lot of punishment.

The Hurricane began as a private venture, with the RAF placing its first orders in June 1936, seven months after its first flight. It was not only the first monoplane fighter in RAF service, but it outnumbered the Spitfire by two to one in the Battle of Britain. It saw service as a light bomber in the Western Desert, a night fighter in the Far East and a convoy protector at sea. It was catapulted off merchant ships (the pilot having to make for a shore base, or ditch near the convoy and be picked up) and served as the Sea Hurricane (the 'Hurricat') on aircraft carriers.

Hurricanes served with air forces around the world, and were produced in Canada in large numbers fitted with American-built Merlin engines. They also saw service in Russia in the form of modified two-seat ground attack aircraft with tandem cockpits.

Although over 14,000 Hurricanes were built (the last, a Mark IV, flew in 1944), the type soon disappeared from RAF service

after the end of World War II. Compared with the Spitfire, which saw service until the late 1950s, very few examples remain today.

Delivered to the Indian Air Force as a Mark IIB, Hurricane AP832 is one that did survive and can be seen in the Air Force Museum at Palam, near New Delhi.

INDIAN AIR FORCE MUSEUM		
OWNER/OPERATOR	:	Indian Air Force
ADDRESS	:	Palam Airport, New Delhi, India
LOCATION	:	9 miles southwest of Delhi
ADMISSION	:	Daily (excluding Tuesday) 1000-1330
FURTHER INFO	:	The aircraft collection is in a hangar on the air force base. A collection of items (uniforms, equipment, documents, etc) depicting the history of the IAF is displayed in a barracks nearby.

Above: One of the few flying examples, this Hurricane belongs to the Canadian Warplane Heritage, Ontario.

Left: The Hurricane at the Indian Air Force Museum.

HAWKER HURRICANE MK1	
COUNTRY OF ORIGIN	**RANGE**
UK	460 miles (740 km)
ENGINES	**CEILING**
Rolls-Royce Merlin II 12 cylinder V air-cooled	33,200 ft (10,120 m)
CREW	**LENGTH**
one	31 ft 5 in (9.55 m)
MAX SPEED	**SPAN**
320 mph (515 km/h) at 20,000 ft (6,100 m)	40 ft 0 in (12.19 m)
	HEIGHT
	13 ft 1 in (3.99 m)

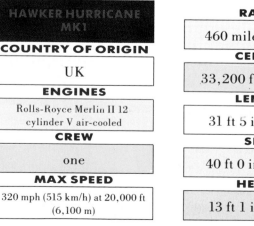

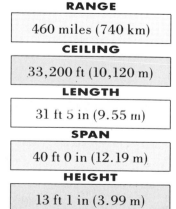

One of the most successful jet fighters ever built, the Hawker Hunter was designed by Sir Sydney Camm, whose work spanned a 40-year period from the Hart biplane fighter of the 1930s, to the VTOL Harrier, and included the Hurricane. The Hunter's clean lines belie the fact that it was a potent fighter aircraft, which in later models was just as useful in the ground attack role. Designed as a replacement for the Gloster Meteor, the prototype made its first flight on 20 July 1951.

As a measure of success, Hunter production ran to nearly 2,000 with over 400 machines being supplied to some 20 countries and 445 built under licence in the Netherlands. Furthermore, more than 700 ex-RAF Hunters were rebuilt for export, mainly to third-world countries.

The prototype, WB188, was modified to F.3 standard and fitted with a Rolls-Royce Avon RA7R. Flown in this form by chief test pilot Neville Duke, it took the air speed record for the UK at a speed of 727.6 mph (1,171.4 km/h).

While WB188 has been preserved in non-flying condition by the RAF Museum, other examples have been purchased by civilians and returned to a flyable state. One such example is operated by Hunter One Collection, and can be seen at air shows throughout Europe, while at least four machines have crossed the Atlantic and are now flying in the United States.

Authentically painted in the colours of No 54 Squadron, RAF, N611JR is operated by Combat Jets Flying Museum of Houston, Texas.

HAWKER HUNTER F.6	
COUNTRY OF ORIGIN	
UK	
ENGINES	
Rolls-Royce Avon 203 turbojet, 10,000 lb (4,536 kg) thrust	
CREW	
one	
MAX SPEED	
710 mph (1,142 km/h)	

RANGE	1,900 miles (3,085 km)
CEILING	51,500 ft (15,700 m)
LENGTH	45 ft 10 in (13.98 m)
SPAN	33 ft 8 in (10.26 m)
HEIGHT	13 ft 2 in (4.01 m)

COMBAT JETS FLYING MUSEUM

OWNER/OPERATOR	:	Jim Robinson
ADDRESS	:	8802 Travellair, Houston, Texas 77061
LOCATION	:	William P Hobby Airport, 7 miles southeast of Houston. Road – Route 35
ADMISSION	:	Prior permission only
FURTHER INFO	:	This private collection of Jet Warbirds also includes an ex-Polish Air Force MiG-15

Main picture: The Hunter at the Combat Jets Flying Museum, painted in the colours of No 54 Squadron RAF.

Inset: At the Aerospace Museum, Shropshire.

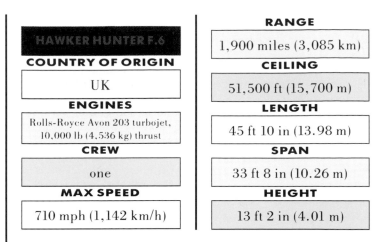

he Sea Fury and its land-based equivalent, the Fury, were designed to meet a British requirement for a long-range fighter suitable for use in the Pacific Theatre of operations. The Fury was cancelled with the end of the war, but the Sea Fury, which had first flown on 21 February 1945, was ordered into production for the Royal Navy, the Admiralty being anxious to fill the gap in performance between the piston-engined Seafire 47 and the introduction of jet aircraft. The first Fleet Air Arm squadron to receive the Sea Fury was No 807, in July 1947, followed by 778, 802, 803 and 805 Squadrons.

In 1948 it was decided to modify the Sea Fury to carry bombs and rockets for the fighter-bomber role with the designation

MUSEO DE PLAYA GIRON		
ADDRESS	:	Playa Giron, Cuba
LOCATION	:	In the town centre
ADMISSION	:	Tuesday-Saturday 1300-1930. Sunday 0930-1300
FURTHER INFO	:	The museum was established to commemorate the Bay of Pigs affair of 1961.

Sea Fury FB.11. Three more Sea Fury squadrons, 801, 804 and 808, had now equipped with the type, and together with 802, 805 and 807 these saw service in the Korean War with the 1st, 17th and 21st Carrier Air Groups aboard the light fleet carriers HMS *Ocean*, HMS *Theseus*, HMS *Glory* and HMAS *Sydney*. The Sea Furies proved extremely effective in the ground attack role, and their pilots also claimed the destruction of two MiG-15 jet fighters.

Sea Furies also served with the Royal Canadian Navy, the Royal Netherlands Navy, the Royal Australian Navy, Pakistan, Burma, Egypt and Cuba. The Burmese aircraft remained operational on counter-insurgency work until the late 1960s, while the Cuban Sea Furies were used to strafe Cuban exiles attempting the abortive 'Bay of Pigs' landing in April 1961.

HAWKER SEA FURY FB.11	RANGE
COUNTRY OF ORIGIN	700 miles (1,130 km)
UK	**CEILING**
ENGINES	36,000 ft (10,970 m)
Bristol Centaurus 18 18-cylinder air-cooled radial, 2,480 hp	**LENGTH**
CREW	34 ft 8 in (10.56 m)
one	**SPAN**
MAX SPEED	38 ft 5 in (11.71 m)
460 mph (740 km/h) at 18,000 ft (5,485 m)	**HEIGHT**
	15 ft 10 in (4.82 m)

On 21 October 1960, Bill Bedford, the chief test pilot of Hawker Aircraft, entered the history books by making the first test flight of the revolutionary P.1127 VTOL (Vertical Take-Off and Landing) aircraft. Three decades later, the Harrier, as the P.1127 became in its developed form, remains the only successful fixed wing VTOL jet combat aircraft in service.

Following the initial flight, five more prototypes were constructed and rigorously tested until the emergence of an improved model, the Kestrel. Nine aircraft were completed and evaluated by an experimental Tripartite Squadron consisting of American, British and German pilots.

After six years of development, the first Harrier flew on 31 August 1966 and, after further testing, entered service with the RAF on 1 April 1969. The same year, the United States finally confirmed their interest, and the Harrier was ordered for the Marine Corps. This was followed by orders from Spain and India for use on their aircraft carriers. Further development resulted in the Sea Harrier for the Royal Navy, first flying on 20 August 1978. The type proved its capability during the Falklands conflict, when 28 Sea Harriers using Sidewinder missiles downed 24 aircraft for no combat loss of their own.

Working with McDonnell Douglas, British Aerospace (who had absorbed Hawker) produced a much-modified Harrier called the Harrier II. Utilizing the same basic engine as the earlier model, the new aircraft was given a new high-lift wing, redesigned jet nozzles and other modifications which resulted in a greatly enhanced performance.

Following the end of the Tripartite trials, six Kestrels were sent to the USA where they were designated XV-6A and continued proving flights. Four remain, including NASA520 at the Aerospace Park, Hampton, Virginia.

AEROSPACE PARK AND INFORMATION CENTRE

OWNER/OPERATOR	:	United States Air Force
ADDRESS	:	413 West Mercury Boulevard, Hampton, Virginia 23666
LOCATION	:	To the north of the city. Road – Route 167
ADMISSION	:	Aircraft: permanent view Information centre: daily 0900-1700
FURTHER INFO	:	The aircraft and missiles are sited in a 15-acre park adjacent to the information centre.

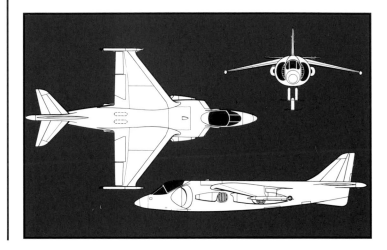

HAWKER P.1127 KESTREL

COUNTRY OF ORIGIN	UK
ENGINES	one Bristol Siddeley Pegasus 5 vectored-thrust turbofan rated at 18,000 lb s t
CREW	one
MAX SPEED	725 mph (1,160 km/h) at 36,000 ft (10,975 m)
RANGE	350 miles (565 km)
CEILING	60,000 ft (18,292 m)
LENGTH	42 ft 6 in (13.70 m)
SPAN	22 ft 11 in (6.97 m)
HEIGHT	10 ft 3 in (3.11 m)

ne flight of one mile (1.61 km), just 33 ft (10 m) above Los Angeles harbour, was the only time the world's largest aircraft ever took to the air. It was a dramatic spectacle for the 50,000 spectators who had gathered to watch the event.

Designed and piloted by Howard Hughes, the 'Spruce Goose' as the H-4 Hercules was nicknamed, made its historic flight on 2 November 1947 before being confined to its specially built hangar for the next 36 years. The vital statistics of the Spruce Goose are impressive when compared to the Boeing 747. Wingspan 124 ft (38.44 m) greater, height 16 ft (4.96 m) greater and length just 13 ft (4.03 m) shorter. Seating capacity was up to 700.

Howard Hughes had conceived the aircraft in 1942 as a troop transport, carrying men and equipment to the various theatres of war, away from the threat of submarines on merchant shipping. The maritime threat diminished, however, and the project was dropped.

After the death of the eccentric billionaire, the Spruce Goose briefly saw the light of day once more. It was moved to a site

QUEEN MARY AND SPRUCE GOOSE

OWNER/OPERATOR	:	Wrather Corporation
ADDRESS	:	Long Beach, California 90801
LOCATION	:	Long Beach Freeway 7 (southern end)
ADMISSION	:	Daily 1000-1800 (0900-2100 July-August)
FURTHER INFO	:	The 'Spruce Goose' is housed in a specially built clear span aluminium dome – the largest in the world. It is surrounded by memorabilia and presentations on the life of Howard Hughes.

alongside the Queen Mary transatlantic liner at Long Beach, and housed in a specially constructed clear span aluminium dome as the focus of an exhibition about Howard Hughes.

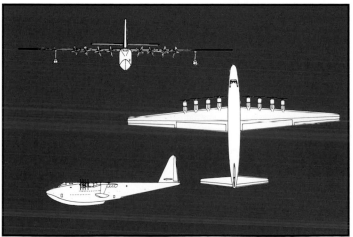

HUGHES H-4 HERCULES		
COUNTRY OF ORIGIN		**RANGE**
USA		3,500 miles (5,633 km)
ENGINES		**CEILING**
eight Pratt & Whitney R-4360 Wasp Major, 28-cylinder radial, air-cooled, 3,000 hp each		n/a
		LENGTH
		219 ft (66.75 m)
CREW		**SPAN**
five		320 ft (97.54 m)
MAX SPEED		**HEIGHT**
175 mph (281 km/h)		79 ft 3 in (24.15 m)

Designed as a tactical light bomber to replace the piston-engined Tupolev Tu-2, Ilyushin's Il-28 formed the mainstay of the Soviet Bloc's tactical air striking forces during the 1950s and was widely exported to other countries within the Soviet sphere of influence. The aircraft was powered by two Klimov VK-1 turbojets, Russian copies of the Rolls-Royce Nene. The first VK-1-powered Il-28 flew on 20 September 1948 and deliveries to units of the Soviet Frontal Aviation began in the following year, the aircraft's simple and robust construction facilitating mass production. Some examples of the Il-28 appeared on Manchurian bases during the Korean War, but these never ventured over the Yalu River and may have been Soviet Air Force machines.

By 1955 some 800 Il-28s were serving with Eastern Bloc air forces. Early recipients were Poland, Czechoslovakia and China, followed by Romania and Hungary. In 1955-56, 60 were delivered to Egypt, about 20 being destroyed at Luxor in an attack by French Air Force F-84F Thunderstreaks during the Suez crisis. Forty more were delivered in 1957. Most of these deliveries involved ex-Czech aircraft, and in 1958 Indonesia received 35 aircraft from a similar source. Some Egyptian Il-28s, flown by Egyptian crews, operated with the Federal Nigerian Air Force during the Biafra War in 1969.

Other countries using the Il-28 were Algeria, Afghanistan, North Vietnam, North Korea and Cuba. The latter's Il-28 deliveries were a leading factor in the crisis of October 1982, which brought the world to the brink of war, and in fact several shipments were turned back by the US naval blockade.

The Ilyushin IL-28 *below*, was designed to replace the Tupolev Tu-2, *above*.

ILYUSHIN IL-28

COUNTRY OF ORIGIN
USSR

ENGINES
two Klimov VK-1 turbojets 6,040 lb (2,740 kg) thrust each

CREW
three

MAX SPEED
559 mph (900 km/h) at 15,000 ft (4,500 m)

RANGE
715 miles (1,135 km)

CEILING
40,355 ft (12,300 m)

LENGTH
57 ft 11 in (17.65 m)

SPAN
70 ft 4 in (21.45 m)

HEIGHT
22 ft 0 in (6.70 m)

Of the 5,000 Junkers Ju 87 Stuka dive bombers built during their reign of terror as they swept across Europe in support of advancing German ground troops during the early stages of World War II, it is incongruous that just two examples remain in existence today.

With little or no aerial resistance over Europe, the Stuka — an abbreviation of the word *Sturzkampfflugzeug,* which simply means 'dive bomber' — was more a psychological weapon than one of physical destruction.

With such a reputation, the German air crews expected the same result when they turned their attention to the south coast of England at the start of what was to become the Battle of Britain. The Hurricanes and Spitfires of the Royal Air Force soon exposed the vulnerability of the dive-bombing concept and the Ju 87 was quickly transferred to ground-attack duties. Notwithstanding its defeat, the Ju 87 was operational long after it had become obsolete and remained in service until as late as the end of 1944.

Although not a particularly successful aircraft — and perhaps one of the ugliest ever built — the Stuka is possibly the best remembered German aircraft of the war after the Messerschmitt Bf 109.

Of the two remaining examples, one is at the Royal Air Force Museum's Battle of Britain Collection at Hendon, near London. The other is at the unlikely venue of the Museum of Science and Industry in Chicago, Illinois, where it is displayed in the company of an early Supermarine Spitfire Mk.1A credited with five kills in 1940/41.

Below : The interior of the Museum of Science and Industry in Chicago.
Bottom: An example of the Ju 87 at the Battle of Britain Museum.

MUSEUM OF SCIENCE AND INDUSTRY

OWNER/OPERATOR	:	Chicago City
ADDRESS	:	57th Street and Lake Shore Drive, Chicago, Illinois 60637
LOCATION	:	4 miles south of the city on the shores of Lake Michigan
ADMISSION	:	Monday-Saturday 0930-1730 (1600 in winter); Sunday 1000-1800
FURTHER INFO	:	The aeronautical collection is spread around the museum which itself is one of the most comprehensive of its type in the world.

JUNKERS Ju-87B-1

COUNTRY OF ORIGIN	
Germany	
ENGINES	
Junkers Jumo 211 12-cylinder V liquid-cooled 1,200 hp	
CREW	
two	
MAX SPEED	
238 mph (383 km/h) at 13,410 ft (4,090 m)	

RANGE	
490 miles (788 km)	
CEILING	
26,250 ft (8,000 m)	
LENGTH	
36 ft 5 in (11.10 m)	
SPAN	
45 ft 3 in (13.79 m)	
HEIGHT	
13 ft 2 in (4.01 m)	

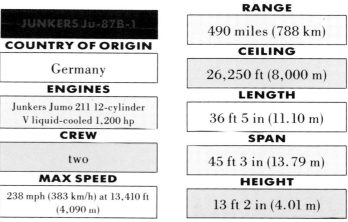

Designed by Professor Richard Knoller, the C.II bomber-reconnaissance aircraft was identical with the earlier C.I with the exception of its engine, which was a more powerful 185 hp Austro-Daimler giving it a maximum speed of 95 mph (152 km/h). One of its main characteristics was its relatively short wingspan of just under 33 ft (9.16 m), a good 10 ft (2.7 m) shorter than that of most other contemporary types designed to perform the same tasks. The C.II equipped several squadrons of the Austro-Hungarian Air Corps from 1916 onwards and was built in Austria by the Lohner, Aviatik and Phönix aircraft factories.

The C.II carried two machine-guns and saw action on both the Russian and Italian fronts. Although it had a higher performance than many other aircraft of its day, it was unstable and unpleasant to fly, and many were lost in landing accidents. One of its best performance features was its rate of climb; it could reach 4,000 ft (1,100 m) in five minutes, above average for its time.

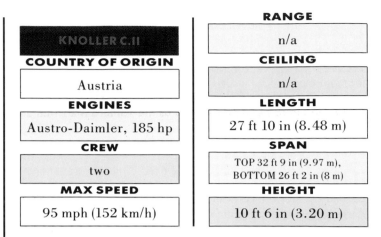

KNOLLER C.II	
COUNTRY OF ORIGIN	**RANGE**
Austria	n/a
ENGINES	**CEILING**
Austro-Daimler, 185 hp	n/a
CREW	**LENGTH**
two	27 ft 10 in (8.48 m)
MAX SPEED	**SPAN**
95 mph (152 km/h)	TOP 32 ft 9 in (9.97 m), BOTTOM 26 ft 2 in (8 m)
	HEIGHT
	10 ft 6 in (3.20 m)

After the end of the war, some C.IIs are reported to have seen service with the embryo Red Air Force and used in action against White Russian forces.

NARODAI TECHNICKE MUZEUM		
ADDRESS	:	Kostelni 42, 170 00 Praha 7, Czechoslovakia
LOCATION	:	In the city centre, north of the river
ADMISSION	:	Daily (excluding Monday) 0900-1700
FURTHER INFO	:	Consisting of seven main departments, the museum's transport collection includes many rare – and sole surviving – types from pre-World War I onwards.

military development of the Model 18 Lodestar civil transport, the Lockheed Ventura was designed to a British requirement for a replacement for the Lockheed Hudson maritime patrol aircraft, then in service with RAF Coastal Command. The first flight was on 31 July 1941 and, in the event, the first deliveries went to RAF Bomber Command, the aircraft entering service as the Ventura Mk I with 21 Squadron of No 2 Group.

The RAF Venturas suffered heavy losses in attacks on targets in the Netherlands, which were mostly made in daylight, and deliveries were halted after about 300 had been supplied. About half of these were Ventura Mk IIs, which had an increased bomb load and uprated engines. The remaining RAF aircraft were allocated to Coastal Command.

About 300 Venturas left over from RAF contracts became B-34A Lexington bombers or B-34B navigational trainers with the USAAF. Subsequent production concentrated on the PV-1 version for the US Navy, ordered in September 1942, which could carry bombs, torpedos or rockets. Total production of the PV-1 was 1,600 aircraft, of which 358 went to RAF Coastal Command and various Commonwealth air forces as the Ventura Mk V.

In RAF service, the Ventura's daylight bombing operations brought the award of the Victoria Cross to a Royal New Zealand Air Force pilot, Squadron Leader L R Trent of 487 Squadron, who pressed on alone to attack a target in Holland after the other 10 aircraft in his formation had been shot down. Trent and his navigator were shot down too, but survived.

SOUTH AFRICAN AIR FORCE MUSEUM	
OWNER/OPERATOR :	South African Air Force
ADDRESS :	AFS Snake Valley, Pretoria, South Africa
LOCATION :	5 miles southeast of Pretoria
ADMISSION :	Prior permission only
FURTHER INFO :	Spread over five locations, the museum collection will be brought together at Swarthop Air Force Base near Pretoria.

LOCKHEED PV-1 VENTURA

COUNTRY OF ORIGIN
USA

ENGINES
two Pratt & Whitney R-2800-31 double Wasp 18-cylinder radial air-cooled, 2,000 hp each

CREW
four/five

MAX SPEED
312 mph (502 km/h) at 13,800 ft (4,200 m)

RANGE
1,600 miles (2,670 km)

CEILING
26,300 ft (8,000 m)

LENGTH
51 ft 9 in (15.77 m)

SPAN
65 ft 6 in (19.96 m)

HEIGHT
11 ft 11 in (3.63 m)

The first jet-propelled combat aircraft to enter service with the USAF, the Shooting Star remained the work-horse of America's tactical fighter-bomber and fighter-interceptor squadrons for five years after the end of World War II, until it was replaced in 1950-51 by more modern types. The prototype flew on 9 January 1944, and in April 1945, two aircraft were shipped to Italy for evaluation under operational conditions, being the only US jet aircraft to see front-line service during the war. Apart from a few short day reconnaissance flights, they saw no action.

The Shooting Star entered service late in 1945 with the 412th Fighter Group. The major production version was the F-80C, and this was still first-line equipment in the summer of 1950, at the outbreak of the Korean War. It equipped six fighter and fighter-bomber groups, and one tactical reconnaissance squadron, in the Pacific area and Japan, and all rendered valu-able service in the war, flying escort missions for B-29s as well as carrying out ground-attack missions on a large scale. The F-80s of the 35th Fighter-Bomber Squadron were the first to see combat, destroying four North Korean Ilyushin Il-10 bombers on 27 June 1950, and on 7 November F-80s of the 51st Fighter Interceptor Wing fought MiG-15s over the Yalu River in history's first jet-versus-jet battle, destroying one of them. With the arrival of Sabres in Korea the Shooting Stars relinquished their fighter role, and by July 1953 only the RF-80Cs of the 67th Tactical Reconnaissance Wing were oper-ational in Korea.

ALAMOGORDO CITY PARK	
OWNER/OPERATOR :	Alamogordo City Council
ADDRESS :	Alamogordo City Park, Alamogordo, New Mexico
LOCATION	
ADMISSION :	Free access
FURTHER INFO :	Alamogordo is 6 miles northeast of the large Holloman Air Force Base which is home to a number of both aircraft and missile units.

Above: The F-80 can also be seen at Robbins Air Force Base Museum of Aviation in Georgia.

LOCKHEED F-80C SHOOTING STAR	
COUNTRY OF ORIGIN	
USA	
ENGINES	
General Electric J33-A-23 turbojet, 4,600 lb (2,086 kg) thrust	
CREW	
one	
MAX SPEED	
580 mph (933 km/h) at 7,000 ft (2,133 m)	
RANGE	
1,380 miles (2,220 km)	
CEILING	
42,750 ft (13,030 m)	
LENGTH	
34 ft 6 in (10.51 m)	
SPAN	
39 ft 11 in (11.85 m)	
HEIGHT	
11 ft 4 in (3.45 m)	

The most widely used advanced trainer in the world, the Lockheed T-33 flew in 1948 and was developed from the F-80 Shooting Star. The type was designated T-33A in USAF service and T-33B (T2-V) with the US Navy and Marine Corps. It is estimated that some 90 per cent of the free world's military jet pilots trained on the T-33 during the 1950s and 1960s. About 5,700 T-33s were built in the USA alone, and others under licence in Canada and Japan. The US Navy's version, the T2-V, entered service in 1957 and featured extensive cockpit redesign. It was used as a deck landing and navigational trainer.

The T-33 served as the USAF's principal advanced trainer for three decades. After 500 hours of ground instruction, student pilots carried out 100 hours of basic flying training and then passed on to a further 75 hours in the T-33 before instruction on fighter aircraft. Although the T-33 has now been replaced in the advanced trainer role by the Cessna T-37, it is still widely used throughout the USAF, where it is familiarly known as the 'T-Bird'. About 200 T-33s are used for combat support, proficiency and radar target illumination training. Student navigators also trained on the T-33 before this task was taken over by the T-37.

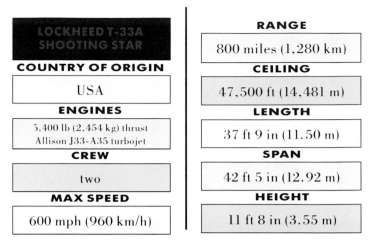

LOCKHEED T-33A SHOOTING STAR	
COUNTRY OF ORIGIN	**RANGE**
USA	800 miles (1,280 km)
ENGINES	**CEILING**
5,400 lb (2,454 kg) thrust Allison J33-A35 turbojet	47,500 ft (14,481 m)
CREW	**LENGTH**
two	37 ft 9 in (11.50 m)
	SPAN
	42 ft 5 in (12.92 m)
MAX SPEED	**HEIGHT**
600 mph (960 km/h)	11 ft 8 in (3.55 m)

WAR MEMORIAL, GJIROKASTER	
ADDRESS	: On the old city ramparts, Gjirokaster, Albania
LOCATION	: Approx 90 miles (145 km) south east of the capital Tirana
ADMISSION	: Daylight hours
FURTHER INFO	: Precise information is difficult to obtain at the present time.

Above: The Shooting Star at the War Museum in Gjirokaster, Albania.
Below: An example on display at the McClellan Aviation Museum, Sacramento, California.

On 5 December 1912, at a dinner given at the Aero Club de France to honour the winner of the Gordon Bennett Aviation race, it was announced that M. Schneider was offering a trophy to the value of F25,000 (approximately £1,000/$1,800) for an international hydro-aeroplane competition.

The Schneider Trophy Races as they came to be known first took place the following year, involving just eight French and one American aircraft. Following the resumption of the Races in 1919 after World War I, they took on an air of national importance for all aviation-minded nations.

Italy, whose aviation industry flourished in the inter-war period, was well represented in the contest throughout this period, with Macchi supplying the majority of their entries.

A number of these aircraft have been preserved, the earliest being a Macchi M.39 of which three were constructed. By far the fastest aircraft present in the 1926 contest which was held at Hampton Roads, Virginia, they came in first and third places (the third entry retired on the 4th lap) averaging 246.5 mph (397 km/h) and 218 mph (351 km/h) respectively.

Four days later, Major Mario de Bernardi, who had piloted the winning aircraft, established a new world speed record of 257 mph (414 km/h).

The aircraft, resplendently restored in its original bright red colour scheme, is on display at the Italian Military Aviation Museum.

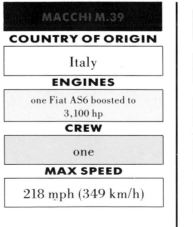

MUSEO STORICO DELL'AERONAUTICA MILITARE ITALIANA	
OWNER/OPERATOR :	Italian Air Force
ADDRESS :	Aeroporto di Vigna di Valle, Vigna di Valle 00062, Italy
LOCATION :	14 miles west of Rome, south of Lago di Bracciano
ADMISSION :	June-September (daily except Monday) 0900-1800; October-May (daily except Monday) 0900-1600
FURTHER INFO :	The museum site covers the historic Luigi Bourlot Airport and Seaplane Base and incorporates two original hangars which, joined by a modern addition, house the majority of the collection.

MACCHI M.39

COUNTRY OF ORIGIN	Italy
ENGINES	one Fiat AS6 boosted to 3,100 hp
CREW	one
MAX SPEED	218 mph (349 km/h)

RANGE	n/a
CEILING	n/a
LENGTH	27 ft 3.6 in (8.32 m)
SPAN	31 ft 1 in (9.47 m)
HEIGHT	10 ft 9.9 in (3.28 m)

On 2 March 1945 the United States Navy placed a contract with the McDonnell Aircraft Corporation for two prototypes of a new naval fighter-bomber design, the XF2D-1. The first of these flew on 11 January 1947 and the first of 56 production F2H-1 Banshees was delivered to Navy Squadron VF-171 in March 1949. In August that year, Lt J L Fruin of VF-171 made the first use in the United States of an ejection seat in a real emergency, ejecting from a Banshee at a speed of over 500 knots.

The F2H-2 was an improved version with an uprated engine and more fuel tankage, and by the time the Korean War broke out in 1950, 334 of these were in service or on order. Operating with squadrons of Task Force 77, the Banshee went into action for the first time on 23 August 1951, when the F2H-2s of VF-172 (USS *Essex*) struck at targets in north-eastern Korea. Two days later, Banshees of the same unit undertook their first fighter escort mission, accompanying B-29s in a high-altitude bombing attack on North Korean marshalling yards at Rashin.

The F2H-3 (redesignated F2-C in 1962) was a long-range limited all-weather fighter development with a lengthened

EL TORO MARINE CORPS AIR STATION	
OWNER/OPERATOR :	United States Marine Corps
ADDRESS :	El Toro, Santa Ana, California 92709
LOCATION :	5 miles east of Los Angeles. Road – Interstate 5
ADMISSION :	Some aircraft on permanent view
FURTHER INFO :	This major marine corps base is home to many units which operate a variety of types.

fuselage, also equipping two squadrons of the Royal Canadian Navy.

The Banshee was retired from first-line US Navy service in September 1959, the last unit to be equipped with it being VAW-11. The Canadian Navy's Banshees remained in service until the mid-1960s.

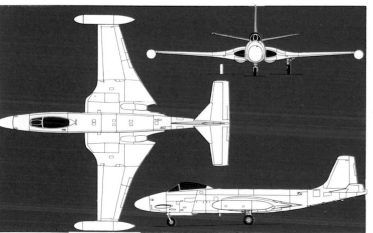

McDONNELL F2H-4 BANSHEE	
COUNTRY OF ORIGIN	
USA	
ENGINES	
two Westinghouse J34-WE-38 turbojets, 3,600 lb (1,633 kg) thrust each	
CREW	
one	
MAX SPEED	
532 mph (856 km/h) at 10,000 ft (3,048 m)	

RANGE
1,475 miles (2,370 km)
CEILING
44,800 ft (13,650 m)
LENGTH
40 ft 2 in (12.25 m)
SPAN
44 ft 10 in (13.66 m)
HEIGHT
14 ft 6 in (4.42 m)

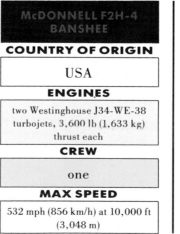

In November 1943 Hitler's overruling command to the Luftwaffe forced them to order the bomber version of the Messerschmitt Me 262, rather than the fighter variant for which it was designed. The decision robbed the German air force of a potent — and much needed — weapon in the later stages of World War II. The Me 262 was Germany's and the world's first jet fighter, and had it been developed earlier, could have inflicted much greater losses to the Allied air forces.

The project had its origins in a request to Messerschmitt from the RLM (the German air ministry) to design a fighter to be powered by the new turbojet engines then under development. The early engines proved unsuitable, and the Me 262 did not fly until 19 July 1942 when the Junkers Jumo engine became available.

Given a very low development priority by the RLM, series production eventually commenced in 1944 as a fighter. Some two months later, Hitler discovered what had occurred, and ordered production to be switched to bombers, all completed airframes to be converted accordingly. Adding further delay and diffusion of effort, other variants were developed to operate in the all-weather fighter, photo-reconnaissance, night fighter and dual-control trainer roles.

As the war was reaching its conclusion, Hitler changed his mind and gave total priority of aircraft production to the Me 262A-1 fighter. It was too late; of some 1,400 Me 262s produced, no more than 100 saw operational service.

Main picture: The Me 262 at the Planes of Fame Air Museum.
Inset: Another example at the Wings of Freedom Air and Space Museum, Pennsylvania.

PLANES OF FAME AIR MUSEUM

OWNER/OPERATOR	:	Ed Maloney
ADDRESS	:	7000 Merrill Avenue, Chino Airport, California 91710
LOCATION	:	7 miles south of Ontario. Road – Route 83
ADMISSION	:	Daily 0900-1700
FURTHER INFO	:	Onee of the major Warbird Airfields in the USA, Chino holds a unique annual show and will hold any aviation buffs for many hours.

MESSERSCHMITT Me 262

COUNTRY OF ORIGIN	
Germany	
ENGINES	
two Junkers Jumo 004B-1, 1,980 lb (898 kg) thrust	
CREW	
one	
MAX SPEED	
540 mph (869 km/h) at 19,685 ft (6,000 m)	

RANGE	
682 miles (1,050 km)	
CEILING	
37,565 ft (11,450 m)	
LENGTH	
34 ft 9.5 in (10.60 m)	
SPAN	
40 ft 11.5 in (12.48 m)	
HEIGHT	
12 ft 7 in (3.84 m)	

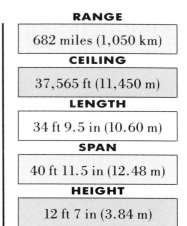

erhaps the most famous jet fighter produced by the Soviet Union, the MiG-15 saw service with the Soviet air force in the Korean War, where it was pitted against the USAF's F-86 Sabre.

Supplied to every Eastern Bloc air force, and many other countries around the world, the second generation MiG-15 had a long and distinguished career once a suitable power plant had been acquired. This occurred in 1946 when, under a new trade agreement and amid much criticism, the British government supplied the USSR with full details and examples of the Rolls-Royce Nene, at that time the world's most advanced jet engine.

The MiG-15 (known to NATO by the code name Fagot) first flew on 30 December 1947 and became operational the following year, remaining in service until the mid-1970s. Over 8,000 examples were produced, which did not include those produced under licence in Czechoslovakia, Poland and the Chinese Republic. In addition to the fighter variants, a tandem two-seat trainer was built in large numbers. Designated the MiG-15UTI (NATO code name Midget), it had the distinction of being the world's first swept-wing jet conversion trainer.

A Chinese-built example in the Military Museum in Peking is displayed in North Korean Air Force markings. It is interesting to note that nine kills are depicted on the side of the aircraft, denoted by red stars – exactly the same symbol used by the USAF pilots at the time to denote Soviet kills.

Two examples of the MiG-15 can be seen in Peking, at the Military Museum Right, *and at the Aeronautical Institute* Below

PEKING MILITARY MUSEUM		
ADDRESS	:	Fuxing Lu, Peking, China
LOCATION	:	5 miles (7 km) west of Tien an Men in the city centre
ADMISSION	:	Prior permission only
FURTHER INFO	:	The aircraft are on display in the open air at the museum, which covers all aspects of Chinese military history.

MIKOYAN-GUREVICH MiG-15
COUNTRY OF ORIGIN
USSR
ENGINES
RD-45F (Rolls-Royce Nene) turbojet, 5,005 lb (2,270 kg) thrust
CREW
one
MAX SPEED
664 mph (1,070 km/h) at 40,000 ft (12,000 m)
RANGE
1,220 miles (1,960 km)
CEILING
50,000 ft (15,200 m)
LENGTH
36 ft 3 in (11.05 m)
SPAN
33 ft 1 in (10.08 m)
HEIGHT
11 ft 2 in (3.40 m)

nown as 'Hound' under the NATO code-name system for Soviet aircraft, the Mi-4, designed by Mikhail L Mil, was similar to America's Sikorsky S-55 but larger. It entered service with the Soviet air force in the summer of 1953 and could carry 14 fully equipped troops. Cargoes of up to 3,500 lb in weight — a 76-mm anti-tank gun, for example — could be loaded into the fuselage through clamshell rear loading doors. Production of the Mi-4 ran into thousands, and the type saw service in many countries as an assault helicopter. Mi-4s serving with the Soviet airline, Aeroflot, were used extensively on internal air networks, and in government service the type was used, among other things, in support of Soviet scientific expeditions to the Arctic and other remote regions.

The Mi-4 was the first helicopter to be built in China, where it was known as the Z-5. It remained in production there for some 20 years, and about 1,000 were built. Some Z-5s were later converted to use the PT6T-6 Turbo Twin Pac engine, developed by Pratt & Whitney Aircraft of Canada.

During its career the Mi-4 established two payload and altitude records in its class. On 26 April 1956 test pilot Yuri Vinizki lifted a load of over 2,000 lb (1,000 kg) to an altitude of 19,958 ft (6,084 m), and on 26 March 1960 this was raised to 24,491 ft (7,466 m) with a similar payload.

VIETNAMESE AIR FORCE MUSEUM		
OWNER/OPERATOR :		Vietnamese Air Force
ADDRESS	:	Ba'u Tang Quan, Chung Ithong Quan, Hanoi, Vietnam
LOCATION	:	In the southern suburbs of the city
ADMISSION	:	Daily
FURTHER INFO	:	The aircraft are on display outside the museum, which contains numerous artefacts, models, etc about the Vietnamese military campaigns.

Main picture: The Mil MI-4 at the Indian Air Force Museum.
Inset: On display at the Vietnamese Air Force Museum.

MIL Mi-4 ('HOUND')
COUNTRY OF ORIGIN
USSR
ENGINES
one Shvetsov ASh-82V 14-cylinder air-cooled radial rated at 1,700 hp for take-off and 1,430 hp maximum continuous rating
CREW
two
MAX SPEED
155 mph (248 km/h)
RANGE
248 miles (396 km)
CEILING
16,000 ft (4,878 m)
LENGTH
53 ft 5 in (16.27 m)
ROTOR DIAMETER
56 ft 6 in (17.22 m)
HEIGHT
17 ft 0 in (5.18 m)

One of the great workhorses of Canada's Arctic wastes and bush, the Norseman was originally produced by Noorduyn Aircraft Ltd, and made its first flight, as a floatplane, on 14 November 1935. Designed by Robert Bernard Cornelius Noorduyn, it was the first Canadian bush plane to have flaps, giving it low take-off and landing speeds to enable it to operate from restricted runways and water bases. In addition, great consideration was given to making the aircraft easy to fly, accessible, and simple to maintain and operate in the spartan bush environment. It could be fitted with wheels, skis or floats.

The Norseman's fabric-covered airframe was built principally of wood, though the fuselage had a strong welded steel tube frame. It was easily repaired, even after major damage or complete immersion in a lake. Its ruggedness suited it to military duties, and Norsemen served in the Royal Canadian Air Force, the RAF, RAAF and the US Army Air Force in World War II – no fewer than 765 serving in the last-named arm as aircrew and navigator trainers, ambulances, transports and cargo carriers.

Total production reached 919 aircraft, manufacturing rights later being acquired by Canadian Car & Foundry Co Ltd. After the war many operators continued to use the Norseman, and surplus military examples were quickly snapped up. It served in many South American countries, and also in Norway, Sweden, Finland, Czechoslovakia, France and Italy. Although a good number have found their way into museums, secondhand and rebuilt examples fetch a high price on the commercial market, where the Norseman's rugged qualities are still greatly prized.

CANADIAN MUSEUM OF FLIGHT AND TRANSPORTATION

ADDRESS	:	13527 Crescent Road, Surrey, British Columbia V4A 2W1
LOCATION	:	South of Vancouver
ADMISSION	:	June-October daily 1100-1500
FURTHER INFO	:	The museum is run by a group of enthusiastic volunteers who have been able to build up an interesting collection including many rare types.

C.C.F. NORSEMAN MK. V

COUNTRY OF ORIGIN	RANGE
USA	464 miles (742 km)

ENGINES	CEILING
one 600 hp Pratt & Whitney R-1340-AN-1 air-cooled radial	17,000 ft (5,182 m)

CREW	LENGTH
one	32 ft 4 in (9.85 m)

	SPAN
	51 ft 8 in (15.74 m)

MAX SPEED	HEIGHT
155 mph (248 km/h)	10 ft 1 in (3.30 m)

Main picture: The Norseman at the National Aviation Museum, Rockcliffe, Ontario.

Inset: The Canadian Museum of Flight and Transportation in British Columbia also includes a Norseman among its exhibits.

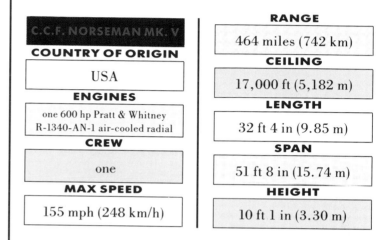

The North American AT-6 began life as the NA-16 which, designed and built for the US Army Air Corps, made its first flight in April 1936. It was the start of a long career which saw over 15,000 produced both in the United States, where it was known as the Texan, and under licence in various other countries.

One of the first American aircraft to be ordered by the RAF, a contract for 200 machines was placed in June 1938 as the standard advanced trainer for the Commonwealth Air Training Scheme. The North American Harvard, as it was known in Britain, was supplied in large numbers to the air forces of Canada, South Africa and Australia.

It was unmistakable by both shape and sound. Noisy and unpleasant to fly, the Harvard nevertheless served with the RAF until 1955. The last pilot trained on the type qualified on 22 March that year.

Postwar, in addition to continued production by the Canadian Car and Foundry Company, more than 2,000 examples were rebuilt as T-6Gs and supplied to over 40 air forces throughout the world. By the time production ended, the AT-6 had entered the history books as having been produced in greater numbers than any other military training aircraft in the western world.

Many examples are still flying today, including two at Britain's Aircraft and Armaments Experimental Establishment (A&AEE). Like many of the RAF Harvards, they were both built under licence by Noorduyn in Canada.

ROYAL NEW ZEALAND AIR FORCE MUSEUM		
OWNER/OPERATOR	:	Royal New Zealand Air Force
ADDRESS	:	Wigram, New Zealand
LOCATION	:	Main South Road, Wigram, near Christchurch
ADMISSION	:	Monday-Friday 1000-1600 Sunday 1300-1600
FURTHER INFO	:	Wigram is an operational Royal New Zealand Air Force Base.

Below The North American AT-6 on display at the Royal New Zealand Air Force Museum.

Below Left: At Boscombe Down, Wiltshire, where it is still operational.

Bottom: Another example at the Castle Air Museum, Atwater, California.

NORTH AMERICAN AT-6A TEXAN/HARVARD
COUNTRY OF ORIGIN
USA
ENGINES
Pratt & Whitney R-1340-49 Wasp 9-cylinder radial, air-cooled, 600 hp
CREW
two
MAX SPEED
208 mph (335 km/h)
RANGE
750 miles (1,025 km)
CEILING
24,200 ft (7,325 m)
LENGTH
29 ft 0 in (8.84 m)
SPAN
42 ft 0 in (12.80 m)
HEIGHT
11 ft 9 in (3.55 m)

The B-25 design was so promising from the outset that the aircraft was ordered into production for the US Army Air Corps (as it was then) without any prototypes being built. The first one flew on 19 August 1940 and 24 had been delivered by the end of the year. These were followed by 40 B-25As, then 119 B-25Bs with dorsal and ventral gun turrets. The first unit to equip with the new bomber was the 17th Bombardment Group.

Production continued with 1,619 B-25Cs and 2,290 B-25Ds, starting early in 1942, and in April that year a formation of Mitchells, flying from the carrier USS *Hornet* and led by Major (later General) James Doolittle, made an historic bombing raid on Tokyo. The B-25G and B-25H were heavily armed 'gunship' versions, mounting a 75-mm cannon and up to 14 machine guns, and these wrought considerable havoc on Japanese shipping in the Pacific War.

The RAF also received 538 Mitchell IIs (B-25Cs and Ds) which equipped a number of bomber squadrons, mostly in Bomber Command's 2 Group. The Soviet Union received 870 Mitchells under Lend-Lease, while others were supplied to Brazil, China and the Netherlands. Some of the latter aircraft were taken over by the Republic of Indonesia and, during the period of confrontation with Malaysia in the early 1960s, carried out leaflet-dropping operations over North Borneo.

The main version of the Mitchell was the B-25J, and a total of 4,318 were completed.

INDONESIAN ARMED FORCES MUSEUM

ADDRESS	:	Jalan Gatot Subroto, Jakarta, Indonesia
LOCATION	:	Between Jakarta and Halim Airport
ADMISSION	:	Daily 1000-1700
FURTHER INFO	:	The aircraft are situated in a park which also contains military vehicles on display.

The Mitchell can be seen around the world. *Top:* In North Weald, Essex, in the UK. *Centre:* On display at Jakarta Armed Forces Museum. *Bottom:* At the Marine Corps Air Ground Museum, Quantico, Virginia.

NORTH AMERICAN B-25H MITCHELL

COUNTRY OF ORIGIN
USA

ENGINES
two Wright R-2600-113 Cyclone 14-cylinder radial air-cooled, 1,700 hp each

CREW
five

MAX SPEED
275 mph (442 km/h) at 13,000 ft (3,960 m)

RANGE
1,350 miles (2,170 km)

CEILING
23,800 ft (7,250 m)

LENGTH
51 ft 0 in (15.54 m)

SPAN
67 ft 7 in (20.60 m)

HEIGHT
15 ft 9 in (4.80 m)

After a speedy, but less than dramatic, start to life in response to an urgent UK requirement for an advanced fighter, the North American Mustang developed into what was arguably the most versatile single-seat fighter of World War II.

In April 1940, the British Purchasing Commission gave North American just 120 days to deliver their proposal in prototype form, which they did with three days to spare. Unfortunately, the lack of a suitable engine delayed the programme and the first aircraft did not fly until 26 October 1940.

While early models were put into service as fighter-reconnaissance machines because of their poor engine performance at higher altitudes, the installation of the American-built Packard Merlin put the Mustang in a class of its own. In their re-engined form, some 1,800 Mustang III and IV were delivered to the RAF for fighter duties, while the USAAF used its ultra-long-range P-51C and P-51D machines as escorts for its daylight bomber formations.

The RAF's Mustangs were withdrawn by the end of 1946, coinciding with the end of a production run of 15,576 aircraft. However, proving that you can't keep a good one down, the P-51 was re-engined with a Rolls-Royce Dart turboprop by Cavalier Aircraft Corp in 1967 as a low-budget performance aircraft, supplying to third-world nations under the United State's Mutual Aid Program.

The fourth prototype XP-51A was seconded to become the first in service with the USAAF for evaluation purposes. Later stored by the National Air and Space Museum, it was acquired by the EAA Foundation with whom it was restored and regularly flown until August, 1982. It now has pride of place in the Warbirds section of their Oshkosh museum.

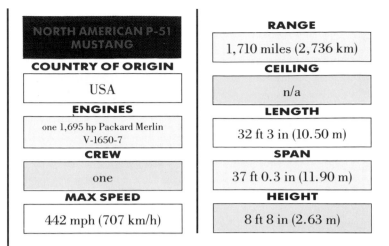

NORTH AMERICAN P-51 MUSTANG	
COUNTRY OF ORIGIN	**RANGE**
USA	1,710 miles (2,736 km)
ENGINES	**CEILING**
one 1,695 hp Packard Merlin V-1650-7	n/a
	LENGTH
	32 ft 3 in (10.50 m)
CREW	**SPAN**
one	37 ft 0.3 in (11.90 m)
MAX SPEED	**HEIGHT**
442 mph (707 km/h)	8 ft 8 in (2.63 m)

EXPERIMENTAL AIRCRAFT ASSOCIATION MUSEUM

OWNER/OPERATOR	:	The Experimental Aircraft Association
ADDRESS	:	3000 Poberezny Road, Wittman Field, Oshkosh, Wisconsin 54903
LOCATION	:	2 miles south of the city
ADMISSION	:	Daily 0830-1700 (Sunday opening 1100)
FURTHER INFO	:	The largest collection of homebuilt aircraft in the world, the museum also features warbirds, aerobatic and air racing aircraft. The 'Pioneer Airport' is a reconstruction of an airfield of the inter-war period.

Main picture: The Mustang at Fort Lauderdale, Florida, in the collection of the Whittington Brothers.
Inset: At the Experimental Aircraft Association in Wisconsin.

Blooded during the Korean conflict, the scene of the first large-scale air warfare between jet-powered aircraft, the North American F-86 Sabre was the first swept-wing jet fighter operated by the United States Air Force.

Considered the best fighter aircraft of its time, the Sabre out-flew and outfought the Russian MiG-15 over Korea even when outnumbered. Fast and very manoeuvrable, it was used by virtually all Western air forces, either new off the production lines or refurbished, and remained in front-line service for over 20 years.

Among its other distinctions, the Sabre became the first aircraft to be adopted as a standard design by NATO. As the F-86K, it was supplied to the air forces of Italy, France, West Germany, the Netherlands and Norway, many of the aircraft being built under licence by Fiat in Italy. Such was the demand for the Sabre that 1,815 were built by Canadair in Canada while others were constructed in Australia and Japan.

While design work started in 1944, the radical concept of a swept wing was not accepted until after the war when German research material had been studied, indicating that it significantly improved high speed performance.

The first prototype, the XF-86, made its maiden flight on 1 October 1947 and the Sabre entered service as the F-86A in February 1949.

Among the many Sabres preserved, an early F-86A is on display at the Selfridge Military Aircraft Museum, Michigan. One of the oldest air bases in the United States, it was named after Lt Thomas Selfridge who, killed in a flying accident with Orville Wright, became the first fatality in powered flight.

SELFRIDGE MILITARY AIR MUSEUM		
OWNER/OPERATOR	:	Michigan Air Guard Historical Association
ADDRESS	:	Selfridge Air Base, Michigan 48045
LOCATION	:	25 miles northeast of Detroit. Road – Interstate 94
ADMISSION	:	April-October Sundays 1300-1700
FURTHER INFO	:	The aircraft are parked outdoors alongside a small indoor exhibition which traces the history of the airfield.

Main picture: The Sabre at the Selfridge Military Museum.
Inset: At the George Air Force Base in California.

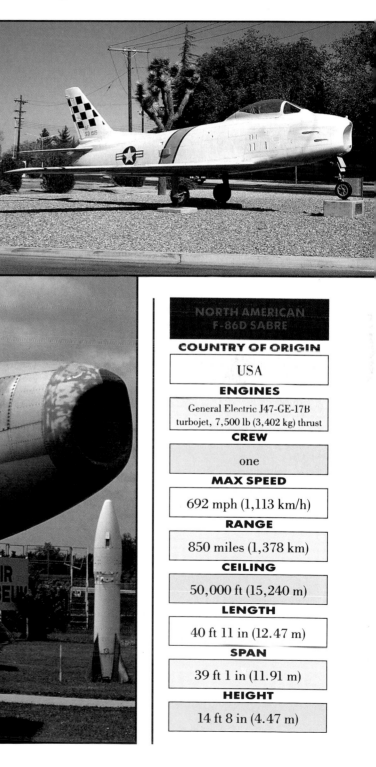

NORTH AMERICAN F-86D SABRE	
COUNTRY OF ORIGIN	
USA	
ENGINES	
General Electric J47-GE-17B turbojet, 7,500 lb (3,402 kg) thrust	
CREW	
one	
MAX SPEED	
692 mph (1,113 km/h)	
RANGE	
850 miles (1,378 km)	
CEILING	
50,000 ft (15,240 m)	
LENGTH	
40 ft 11 in (12.47 m)	
SPAN	
39 ft 1 in (11.91 m)	
HEIGHT	
14 ft 8 in (4.47 m)	

he futuristic lines of the North American XB-70 Valkyrie belie the fact that it was designed in the early 1960s as a replacement for the Boeing B-52 strategic bomber. In practice, military thinking at the time was directed towards using intercontinental ballistic missiles in the role and as a result only two prototypes were built.

Unparalleled as the largest and most complex research aircraft ever built, the prototype XB-70A made its maiden flight on 21 September 1964. Originally designed to fly up to 7,600 miles (12,230 km) unrefuelled, at a constant speed in excess of Mach 3, it incorporated both unusual design features and materials.

Featuring a canard delta wing arrangement, the Valkyrie had a long slim titanium fuselage above the wing, and a broad rectangular engine nacelle beneath. A unique feature was the wing design whereby the outer sections hinged down 25 degrees for low-level supersonic flight and 65 degrees for Mach 3 flights at high-altitude.

Virtually all of the test flying was undertaken by the first prototype. Early in the test programme, the second prototype was lost when it collided with a F-104 Starfighter photographic chase aircraft on 8 June 1966 with the loss of both crews.

Having reached a top speed of Mach 3.08 and altitude of 73,980 ft (22,550 m), the XB-70A Valkyrie made its last flight on 4 February 1969.

UNITED STATES AIR FORCE MUSEUM	
OWNER/OPERATOR :	United States Air Force
ADDRESS :	Wright Patterson Air Force Base, Dayton, Ohio 45433
LOCATION :	4 miles northeast of Dayton. Road – Highway 4
ADMISSION :	Monday-Friday 0900-1700 (annex 0930-1500) Saturday-Sunday 1000-1800 (annex 1030-1700)
FURTHER INFO :	The museum has the largest collection of aircraft in the world, although many aircraft are loaned to other museums in the USA and abroad and therefore not on show.

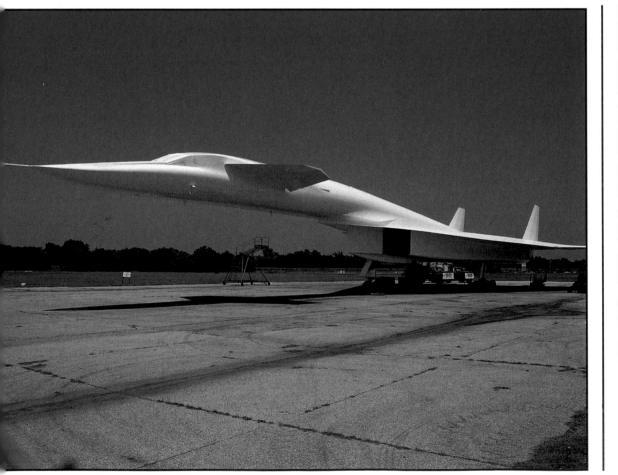

NORTH AMERICAN XB-70A VALKYRIE

COUNTRY OF ORIGIN
USA

ENGINES
six General Electric YN93-GE-3 turbojets, 31,000 lb (14,060 kg) thrust (with afterburning each)

CREW
two

MAX SPEED
mach 3

RANGE
7,600 miles (12,230 km)

CEILING
73,980 ft (22,550 m)

LENGTH
196 ft 0 in (59.64 m)

SPAN
105 ft 0 in (32 m) tips spread

HEIGHT
30 ft 0 in (9.14 m)

When Poland's State Aviation Works was founded in Warsaw at the end of 1927, designer Ing Zygmunt Pulawski set to work on a series of outstanding monoplane fighters featuring a high-set strut-braced gull wing which allowed the pilot a perfect view for air combat. This concept reached its acme in the P-11, powered by the licence-built Bristol Mercury radial engine. The first prototype of this attractive fighter made its maiden flight in September 1931, powered by a Bristol Jupiter. The first production batch, comprising 30 aircraft, was completed in one year — 1934 — and total P-11 production ran to 250 units.

The P-11's fuselage was a stressed-skin duralumin structure, while the wing had a duralumin framework and was mostly covered with corrugated duralumin sheet. The long, narrow-chord ailerons could double as flaps to reduce landing speeds. The v-strutted fixed landing gear was exceptionally strong. Basic armament was a pair of 0.3 calibre KM Wz33 machine guns with 500 rounds each, fitted in the fuselage sides and firing through the propeller arc.

On September 1 1939, when Hitler's invading forces swept into Poland, the Polish Air Force was outnumbered nine to one by the Luftwaffe, whose equipment was far superior. Nonetheless, the Polish Air Force put up dogged resistance for 17 days, losing 333 of its 430 front-line aircraft. At the forefront of this desperate battle was the P-11C, now obsolete but highly manoeuvrable and flown by courageous pilots. Despite heroic efforts, the superior force prevailed, and on September 17 the remaining 38 P-11s and P-7s (an earlier type) were evacuated to Rumania.

MUZEUM LOTNICTURA I ASTRONAUTYKI	
ADDRESS :	30-969 Krakov 28, Poland
LOCATION :	3 miles east of the city at the disused Rakowice airfield. Road – Route E22
ADMISSION :	May-October 1000-1400
FURTHER INFO :	The museum includes the survivors from the famous Deutsche Luftfahrtsammlung (Berlin Air Museum) which was destroyed in an air raid.

PZL P-11	
COUNTRY OF ORIGIN	
Poland	
ENGINES	
Gnome-Rhone 14 N7 14-cylinder radial air-cooled 930 hp	
CREW	
one	
MAX SPEED	
254 mph (408 km/h) at 14,763 ft (4,490 m)	

RANGE	
497 miles (800 km)	
CEILING	
29,527 ft (9,000 m)	
LENGTH	
24 ft 7.5 in (7.52 m)	
SPAN	
35 ft 2 in (10.75 m)	
HEIGHT	
8 ft 10 in (2.70 m)	

Unquestionably one of the great fighters of World War II, the 'Jug', as it was affectionately known, was designed by Alexander Kartveli to meet a United States Army Air Force requirement for a 'super fighter'. It first flew on 6 May, 1941 as the XP-47B, a rotund six-ton giant of a fighter spanning 40 ft and powered by a supercharged 2,000 hp Pratt & Whitney radial engine.

Although the Thunderbolt had none of the sleek elegance of its European counterparts, it soon proved to be an agile and doughty opponent.

Under the pressures of war, development proceeded apace. The P-47C, which appeared late in 1942, could carry a ventral fuel tank and also had increased internal fuel capacity to increase the type's range. In combat over Europe, the Thunderbolt soon began to give a good account of itself, providing valuable service as a bomber escort.

In 1943 the P-47D came into service, this development having water injection to coax another 300 hp from the engine, and paddle-bladed propellers. To improve all-round visibility, a bubble canopy was introduced on later P-47Ds; the rear fuselage top-decking was cut down to accommodate this. Later in the year the Thunderbolt came to be used as a fighter-bomber – a role in which it excelled.

The 'Jug' subsequently served in nearly all of the war theatres, and served with the RAF, the Free French and the Russians. The ultimate version was the long-range P-47N, with redesigned wings, for service in the Pacific theatre. Production of all variants totalled 15,683 aircraft, and P-47s were credited with the destruction of more than 7,000 enemy aircraft, 3,753 of these in aerial combat.

NEW ENGLAND AIR MUSEUM	
OWNER/OPERATOR :	Connecticut Aeronautical Historical Association
ADDRESS :	Bradley International Airport, Windsor Locks, Connecticut 06096
LOCATION :	North side of the airport. Road – Route 75
ADMISSION :	Daily 1000-1700
FURTHER INFO :	Approximately 40 aircraft are displayed in the exhibition hall of the museum which is becoming one of the major aviation museums in the USA.

Left: The Thunderbolt at the New England Air Museum.
Below: Another example at the Lone Star Flight Museum in Houston, Texas.

REPUBLIC P-47D THUNDERBOLT	
COUNTRY OF ORIGIN	USA
ENGINES	Pratt & Whitney R-2800-59 double Wasp 18-cylinder radial air-cooled, 2,535 hp
CREW	one
MAX SPEED	428 mph (689 km/h) at 30,000 ft (9,150 m)
RANGE	475 miles (765 km)
CEILING	42,000 ft (12,800 m)
LENGTH	36 ft 2 in (11 m)
SPAN	40 ft 9 in (14.42 m)
HEIGHT	14 ft 2 in (4.31 m)

rivate flying was slow to develop in Denmark, but in 1937 a small single-seat monoplane, the KZ I, was produced by Viggo Kramme and K G Zeuthen. Subsequently financial backing was obtained and the Skandinavisk Aero Industri A/S was formed. The new company's first product was the KZ II Kupe, a two-seat low-wing monoplane in which the two occupants were seated side-by-side in an enclosed cockpit.

Built of wood and welded steel tube, with fabric covering, the KZ II could be powered by either a 90 hp Cirrus Minor or a 90 hp de Havilland Gypsy Minor. The prototype made its maiden flight at Kastrup on 11 December 1937, piloted by Arvid Hansen. Production of the Kupe ran to 14 aircraft, most of which went to Danish owners, but three went to Sweden and one to Switzerland.

An open-cockpit tandem version, the KZ II Sport powered by the 105 hp Hirth HM 504A II, appeared in 1938, and of the 11 completed, four went to the Danish Naval Air Service.

After the war KZ II production was resumed, and an improved version, the KZ II Traener, was introduced. This was similar to the Sport, but had a strengthened airframe and slotted wing tips. The first of the line, which made its maiden flight in April 1946, was fitted with an enclosed canopy, but production aircraft had an open cockpit.

The Danish Air Force bought 15 Traeners. The prototype and first six production aircraft had the 130 hp de Havilland Gypsy Major I, but the remainder were fitted with the 145 hp Gypsy Major X. The Air Force's Traeners were declared surplus in 1953 and sold on the civil market. Subsequently most of them were given canopies, and other modifications were made to improve comfort or enhance performance. Several KZ IIs of various types are still flying today.

DANSK VETERANFLYSAMLUNG	
OWNER/OPERATOR :	Kz Veteranfly Klubber
ADDRESS :	Stauning Lufthavn, Skjern 6900, Denmark
LOCATION :	45 miles north of Esbjerg between Ringkobing and Skern
ADMISSION :	Sunday or prior permission weekday
FURTHER INFO :	Flying displays are held on the last Sunday of the month in June, July and August.

SKANDINAVISK AERO INDUSTRI KZ II KUPE

COUNTRY OF ORIGIN	
Denmark	

ENGINES	
one 130 hp de Havilland Gypsy Major air-cooled inline	

CREW	
one	

MAX SPEED	
146 mph (235 km/h)	

RANGE	
n/a	

CEILING	
16,400 ft (5,084 m)	

LENGTH	
24 ft 7 in (7.63 m)	

SPAN	
33 ft 6 in (10.39 m)	

HEIGHT	
7 ft 4.5 in (2.29 m)	

Designed as a tough, multi-purpose feederliner or military transport aircraft capable of operating from small fields, the Twin Pioneer first flew at Prestwick on 25 June 1955. Powered by a pair of Alvis Leonides radial engines, it was a sturdy high-wing monoplane with triple fins and rudders and a fixed undercarriage, able to carry a crew of two and 16 passengers. All-metal stressed-skin construction was used, and the wings had leading edge slats and Fowler flaps which gave it outstanding short take-off and landing abilities.

Initial sales were made to civil operators around the world, in such diverse countries as Mexico, Austria, Switzerland, Kuwait, Iraq, Nigeria and the Philippines. The first of 39 Twin Pioneers for the RAF flew in August 1957. Of these aircraft, the first 32 were designated C.C.1, and the last seven, which differed structurally, were designated Twin Pioneer C.C.2.

Deliveries to the RAF began in 1958 and were completed in March 1961. They served in Bahrein, Kuwait, Kenya and Borneo before the type was withdrawn from front-line duties at the end of 1968.

In the Far East four Twin Pioneers served with Borneo Airways, and three with de Kroonduif, a Dutch company based in the Netherlands East Indies, these aircraft later transferring to Garuda Indonesian Airways. Another 12 served with the Royal Malayan Air Force, the first to be delivered, FM1001, also being the RMAF's first aircraft. They served in the RMAF from April 1958 to 1970, when all but one of them were sold to Aerial Agriculture in Australia. The remaining aircraft, FM1001, is now displayed in the grounds of the Malaysian National Museum, in Kuala Lumpur city centre. A total of 87 Twin Pioneers was built, production ceasing in 1963.

MUZIUM NEGARA		
ADDRESS	:	Jalan Damansara, Kuala Lumpur, Malaysia
LOCATION	:	In the city centre
ADMISSION	:	Daily 0900-1200
FURTHER INFO	:	The Twin Pioneer is in the grounds of the Malaysian National Museum which details the history and culture of the country.

Examples of the Scottish Twin Pioneer are on display at the Malaysian National Museum *top*, and at the Aerospace Museum in Shropshire *bottom*.

SCOTTISH AVIATION TWIN PIONEER	
COUNTRY OF ORIGIN	UK
ENGINES	two Alvis Leonides 531/8 9-cylinder air-cooled radials each rated at 640 hp
CREW	two
MAX SPEED	160 mph (256 km/h) at 2,500 ft (762 m)
RANGE	800 miles (1,280 km) at econ. cruising speed
CEILING	18,000 ft (5,487 m)
LENGTH	45 ft 3 in (14.46 m)
SPAN	76 ft 6 in (23.32 m)
HEIGHT	12 ft 3 in (4.40 m)

In 1933 the British Air Ministry issued a requirement for a four-engined monoplane flying-boat for long-range reconnaissance and anti-submarine duties. Short Brothers Ltd submitted its S.25 design, developed from the 'C'-Class Empire flying-boat, and the prototype, now named the Sunderland, first flew on 16 October 1937. The first British flying-boat to have power-operated gun turrets, the Sunderland entered RAF service in the summer of 1938 with 230 Squadron at Singapore and 210 Squadron at Pembroke Dock in South Wales.

Coastal Command had only three Sunderland squadrons when war broke out, but by early 1943 there were nine. The aircraft quickly gained a notable reputation, and because of its formidable defensive armament it became known to the Germans as the 'Flying Porcupine'. Throughout the war the Sunderland performed outstanding work on anti-submarine and convoy escort patrols over the Atlantic, the North Sea, the Mediterranean and the Indian Ocean, and played a significant part in the evacuations of Norway, Greece and Crete.

By the time production ended, in June 1946, 739 had been built in several marks. After the war Sunderlands served as transports in the Berlin Airlift, and flew 1,647 operational sorties in the Korean War, based in Japan. They also attacked Malayan terrorists, and performed a series of airlifts in support of the British North Greenland Expedition of 1951-54.

The last flying-boat in RAF service, the Sunderland was finally retired on 15 May 1959. This famous aircraft also served with the French Aeronavale from 1951 to 1960, and with the Royal New Zealand Air Force from 1953 to 1967. The example depicted is the NZ4115, now preserved at the Museum of Transport and Technology in Auckland.

MUSEUM OF TRANSPORT AND TECHNOLOGY	
ADDRESS	: Great North Road, Western Springs, Auckland 2, New Zealand
LOCATION	: 2 miles southwest of the city centre
ADMISSION	: Daily 0900-1700
FURTHER INFO	: The museum represents all types of transport and holds regular 'live' weekends. The main site is connected by a tramway to a 20-acre park where the larger aircraft are exhibited.

Left: The Short S.25 Sunderland.
Below: The civilian Short S.25 Sandringham.

SHORT SUNDERLAND MK1

COUNTRY OF ORIGIN
UK

ENGINES
four Bristol Pegasus XXII 9-cylinder radial air-cooled, 1010 hp each

CREW
thirteen

MAX SPEED
210 mph (338 km/h) at 6,500 ft (2,000 m)

RANGE
2,980 miles (4,800 km)

CEILING
17,900 ft (5,500 m)

LENGTH
85 ft 4 in (26.00 m)

SPAN
112 ft 9 in (34.35 m)

HEIGHT
32 ft 10 in (10.00 m)

Probably the only single-seat aeroplane to have five engines, the S.C.1 resulted from a specification issued by Britain's Ministry of Supply, calling for a research aeroplane able to take off using jet lift alone, accelerate into forward flight and then decelerate to zero forward speed and alight vertically under jet lift. The submission by Short Brothers of Belfast had a battery of four Rolls-Royce RB.108 turbojets to provide the vertical thrust, and a single RB.108 in the rear fuselage for propulsion. The pilot, who was provided with conventional controls plus throttle and tilt levers for the lift engines, was accommodated in a bulbous cockpit in the nose, and the aircraft had a small delta wing and a stalky fixed tricycle undercarriage. Stability in hovering flight was provided by valves in the nose, tail and wingtips, using air bled from the engines.

The first of the two S.C.1s built began trials in December 1956 and made its first conventional take-off and landing on 2 April 1957. The first tethered hovering flight was made by the second machine on 23 May, 1958, and the first free hovering flight followed on 25 October. The first in-flight transition from level flight to hover and back again occurred on 6 April 1960, and from then onwards both S.C.1s were engaged in a busy routine of test flights and modifications as the techniques were refined. The first full transition in public was made at the 1960 Farnborough show.

Eventually the advent of the Pegasus engine and the Hawker P.1127 rendered the concept obsolete, and both S.C.1s were withdrawn from use, having provided extensive and valuable data. The first machine, XG900, is displayed at Yeovilton, and the second, XG905, is in the Ulster Folk and Transport Museum in Northern Ireland.

ULSTER FOLK AND TRANSPORT MUSEUM		
OWNER/OPERATOR	:	Belfast Transport Museum
ADDRESS	:	Cultra Manor, Holywood, County Down, Northern Ireland
LOCATION	:	7 miles northeast of Belfast. Road – A2
ADMISSION	:	May-September 1100-1900 October-April 1100-1700 Opens at 1400 on Sundays
FURTHER INFO	:	Built locally by Short Bros, the S.C.1 shares the museum with other aircraft types as well as many local buildings transferred to the site to illustrate the rural history of the province.

SHORT S.C.1
COUNTRY OF ORIGIN
UK
ENGINES
five Rolls-Royce RB.108 turbojet engines (each 2,130 lb (966 kg s t) fuel in leading-edge tank and bag-type inter-spar tank in each wing
CREW
one
MAX SPEED
246 mph (393.6 km/h)
RANGE
n/a
CEILING
n/a
LENGTH
29 ft 10 in (9.11 m)
SPAN
23 ft 6 in (7.16 m)
HEIGHT
10 ft 8 in (3.25 m)

n June 1952 the United States Navy ordered a new anti-submarine helicopter from Sikorsky Aircraft. The helicopter was given the manufacturer's designation S-58, and the US Navy designation XHSS-1. The prototype made its maiden flight on 8 March 1954, heralding a long production run of more than 2,250 aircraft by Sikorsky alone.

The S-58 was powered by a 1,525 hp Wright R-1820 radial piston engine, mounted obliquely in the nose. This allowed the transmission shaft to run at right angles to the engine, straight into the gearbox beneath the hub of the four-bladed main rotor. To facilitate stowage on board ship, the rotor blades could be folded aft, while the rear fuselage and tail rotor folded forward.

The majority of S-58s were built for military use, but the type also served as a commercial transport, carrying up to 18 passengers. Operators included Sabena and Chicago Helicopter

Airways. The 350 S-58s supplied to the US Navy were originally designated HSS Seabat, and the 603 built for the US Marines were HUS Seahorse. Later, both were redesignated H-34, this identity covering a range of variants developed for specific tasks.

The US Army also ordered the S-58, and the H-34 Choctaw soon became the Service's principal transport helicopter. Other nations which equipped their forces with the S-58 included Japan and West Germany, while 135 were built under licence by Aerospatiale of France and 365 by Westland in Great Britain. These served with the Royal Navy as the Wessex, also doing duty with the Royal Marines and Royal Air Force. The Wessex had a 1,450 hp Napier Gazelle turbine in place of the S-58's Wright radial.

The S-58 undertook many other duties, such as search and rescue, casualty evacuation, support and ground attack, and even VIP transport.

SIKORSKY S-58		RANGE
COUNTRY OF ORIGIN		384 miles (614 km)
USA		**CEILING**
ENGINES		4,000 ft (1,219 m)
one 1,525 hp Wright R-1820-84 piston-engine		**LENGTH**
CREW		47 ft 2 in (14.37 m)
two		**ROTOR DIAMETER**
MAX SPEED		56 ft 0 in (17.07 m)
123 mph (196 km/h)		**HEIGHT**
		15 ft 10 in (4.75 m)

LUFTWAFFEN MUSEUM	
OWNER/OPERATOR :	Luftwaffe
ADDRESS :	Fliegerhorst Uetersen, Uetersen 2082, Germany
LOCATION :	20 km northwest of Hamburg. Roads – between Roads no 5 and no 431
ADMISSION :	Daily – but check first
FURTHER INFO :	The museum is in two hangars on the north side of this non-flying military base. It traces the history of the Luftwaffe up to the present day.

Main picture: The Sikorsky S-58 in the Luftwaffe Museum. *Inset*: Civilian Wessex disguised as a US Marine S-58 at the International Helicopter Museum, Avon.

In 1933, one of the world's greatest primary trainers, the Kaydet, began life as the Stearman Model 70, an open-cockpit tandem two-seat biplane aimed at US Army and US Navy requirements. Its most conspicuous feature was its simple single undercarriage legs.

This prototype spawned a whole family of highly successful trainers, by far the most prolific of which was the Model 75 Kaydet, which first went into production for the US Army in 1936. Three years later the Stearman Aircraft Company of Wichita, Kansas, became a division of Boeing, and most Model 75s were built during World War II. A grand total of 8,584 Boeing-Stearmans in the 70-76 series was built, with spares components bringing the figure up to 10,346 aircraft. Thousands of US military pilots were fledged on them and they served in the US Army as the PT-13, 17, 18 and 27, and in the US Navy as the N2S, powered by various radial engines of 220 hp. Production ceased in 1944.

Many other nations used the Model 75 as their basic military trainer, among them Canada, China, Cuba, Brazil, Bolivia, Columbia, Guatemala, Argentina, Venezuela, Peru, the Dominican Republic and the Philippines.

Post-war, many Model 75s entered the civil market, often being fitted with more powerful engines and serving as single-seat crop dusters and sprayers. In 1950 no fewer than 4,125 Model 75s were still on the US civil register, but the number had dwindled to 2,028 in 1959. Since then its value as an antique has been appreciated, and many have been restored to their original configuration.

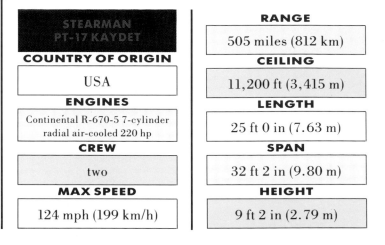

MUSEO AERONAUTICO

OWNER/OPERATOR	:	Chilean Air Force
ADDRESS	:	Quinta Normal, Santiago
LOCATION	:	In the western suburbs of the city
ADMISSION	:	Weekends only
FURTHER INFO	:	Although part of the museum, the Kaydet is actually based at the nearby El Bosque Air Base.

STEARMAN PT-17 KAYDET

COUNTRY OF ORIGIN	RANGE
USA	505 miles (812 km)

ENGINES	CEILING
Continental R-670-5 7-cylinder radial air-cooled 220 hp	11,200 ft (3,415 m)

CREW	LENGTH
two	25 ft 0 in (7.63 m)

	SPAN
	32 ft 2 in (9.80 m)

MAX SPEED	HEIGHT
124 mph (199 km/h)	9 ft 2 in (2.79 m)

he Vautour (Vulture) was the product of designer Jean Charles Parot and his team at SNCA de Sud-Ouest, designed to meet a 1951 French Air Staff specification for a versatile twin-jet aircraft which could be used in the all-weather fighter, close support, light bomber, and reconnaissance roles. With its 35° swept wing, underslung SNECMA Atar turbojets, tandem twin-wheel main undercarriage and stabilizing auxiliary wheels housed in the engine nacelles, it was a distinctive and advanced machine for its time.

The first prototype, configured as a two-seat night fighter, made its maiden flight on 16 October 1952 and later exceeded the speed of sound in a shallow dive. The second prototype, a single-seat ground-attack aircraft, flew on December 4 1953, and the third, the bomber variant, flew a year later. The French Air Staff ordered 300 Vautour IIA single-seat attack aircraft, 140 Vautour IIN night and all-weather fighters, and 40 Vautour IIB bombers. The IIAs were cancelled in 1957, only 30 being flown, and 25 were sold to Israel in 1960; only 70 IINs were built, these being delivered to the Armée de l'Air in 1956-59; all 40 IIBs were produced and formed the nucleus of the Armée de l'Air's deterrent force, the Commandement des Forces Aériennes Strategiques. The final Vautour variant, the IIBR bomber-reconnaissance aircraft, did not go into production.

The last Vautours in service in France were the II.1Ns of the 30e Escadre at Reims, which were replaced by Mirage F1.Cs in the mid-1970s. The Israeli IIAs were withdrawn from combat duty after the October 1973 war, some being converted to carry electronic countermeasures.

BASE AERIENNE REIMS		
OWNER/OPERATOR :		L'Armée de l'Air
ADDRESS	:	Reims/Champagne Base Aerienne, Reims, France
LOCATION	:	4 miles (6 km) north of Reims
ADMISSION	:	On view at entrance
FURTHER INFO	:	Reims/Champagne is an operational French Air Force base.

SUD-OUEST S.O. VAUTOUR	
COUNTRY OF ORIGIN	**RANGE**
France	3,728 miles (5,964 km)
ENGINES	**CEILING**
two 7,716 lb st (3,506 kg) SNECMA Atar turbojets	44,290 ft (13,503 m)
CREW	**LENGTH**
one/two	51 ft 1 in (15.56 m)
MAX SPEED	**SPAN**
720 mph (1,152 km/h)	49 ft 6.5 in (15.09 m)
	HEIGHT
	14 ft 1 in (4. 26 m)

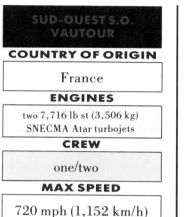
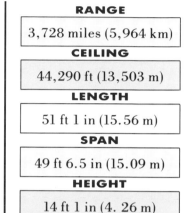

No aircraft in the history of aviation has stirred the imagination as much as the Supermarine Spitfire. The symbol of the superiority of the Royal Air Force over the might of the German Luftwaffe during the Battle of Britain, the Spitfire was a thoroughbred classic aeroplane. Designed to the same Air Ministry specification as the Hawker Hurricane, it incorporated many design features from the Supermarine S-6B seaplane which had won the Schneider Trophy outright for Britain.

While both companies' designs adequately met the specifications, the two chief designers looked at the requirements from completely different angles. It has been said that, while Sydney Camm of Hawker produced a solid war-horse capable of taking considerable punishment, Supermarine's Mitchell designed a ballerina.

ISRAELI AIR FORCE HISTORIC COLLECTION	
OWNER/OPERATOR :	Israeli Air Force
ADDRESS :	Hatzerim Air Force Base, Neger, Israel
LOCATION :	South of Beersheeba
ADMISSION :	Stricly prior permission only
FURTHER INFO :	Hatzerim AFB is home of the Israeli Air Force's flying school which operates both fixed and rotary wing aircraft.

Below right: The Spitfire can also be seen at the Imperial War Museum in London.

SUPERMARINE SPITFIRE MK 1
COUNTRY OF ORIGIN
UK
ENGINES
Rolls-Royce Merlin II 12-cylinder V liquid-cooled, 1,030 hp
CREW
one
MAX SPEED
355 mph (571 km/h) at 19,000 ft (5,800 m)
RANGE
500 miles (805 km)
CEILING
34,000 ft (10,360 m)
LENGTH
29 ft 11 in (9.12 m)
SPAN
36 ft 10 in (11.22 m)
HEIGHT
11 ft 5 in (3.48 m)

The history of the Spitfire has been well documented, and requires little repetition. It fought in virtually every theatre of World War II, and remained in military service into the 1960s. From entering service in 1938, the design was constantly developed so that by the time production ended in October 1947, 20,351 aircraft in some 40 different variants had been produced — more than any other British aircraft type.

A relatively large number of Spitfires survive, and many are being rebuilt to flying condition. An interesting example is the 'Black Spitfire', former personal mount of Ezer Wiezman, chief of the Israel air force, which is still in flying condition. Now preserved at the IAF museum at Beersheba, it was previously with the Czech Air Force.

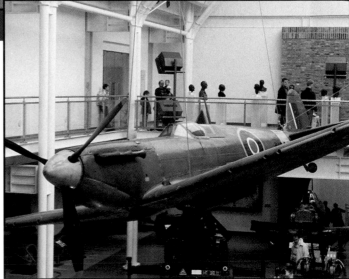

requirement for a two-seat, single-engined army co-operation monoplane was issued by the Japanese military authorities in 1937. It was to be extremely manoeuvrable at low altitudes, and able to operate from rough airstrips close to the front line. Radio and photographic equipment, and racks for light anti-personnel bombs were to be carried.

Two designs tendered to the specification were duly considered, and Tachikawa Hikoki KK was instructed to build prototypes of its proposal, the Ki-36, designed under the leadership of Ryokichi Endo. The Ki-36 was a low-wing, radial-engined monoplane with a fixed, spatted undercarriage. The swept-back leading edge of its wing allowed the pilot a good forward and downward view, and transparent panels were in the wing centre section beneath the fuselage.

The first Ki-36 prototype made its maiden flight on 20 April 1938, at Tachikawa, and proved to have a brisk take-off and a sprightful performance. Armament comprised a single forward-firing 7.7 mm Type 89 machine gun within the engine cowling, and a similar weapon on a movable mounting.

Production started in November 1938, the aircraft being known as the Army Type 98 Direct Co-operation Plane. During the second Sino-Japanese conflict, Ki-36s were used with success in small detachments assigned to Japanese Army units. In the Pacific in World War II, however, they were out-classed by Allied fighters and were relegated to China. Thailand took delivery of a small number of Ki-36s, the example depicted being one of these.

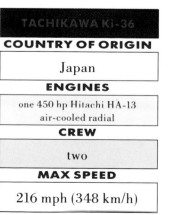

Above: The Tachikawa Ki-36 at the Royal Thai Air Force Museum. An example of the Ki-55 (right) is at the Peking Military Museum.

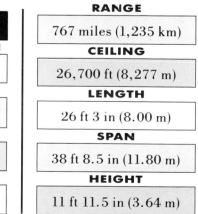

ROYAL THAI AIR FORCE MUSEUM

OWNER/OPERATOR :	Royal Thai Air Force
ADDRESS :	Don Muang Air Force Base, Bangkok, Thailand
LOCATION :	15 miles northeast of the city on the Polyothin Road
ADMISSION :	Monday-Friday 0830-1630 (Closed 1200-1300). First weekend in the month 0900-1700 (closed 1200-1400)
FURTHER INFO :	The museum is perhaps the most important aviation collection in Asia. It houses a comprehensive display of models and memorabilia while the aircraft are restored to a high standard.

TACHIKAWA Ki-36

COUNTRY OF ORIGIN	
Japan	
ENGINES	
one 450 hp Hitachi HA-13 air-cooled radial	
CREW	
two	
MAX SPEED	
216 mph (348 km/h)	

RANGE	
767 miles (1,235 km)	
CEILING	
26,700 ft (8,277 m)	
LENGTH	
26 ft 3 in (8.00 m)	
SPAN	
38 ft 8.5 in (11.80 m)	
HEIGHT	
11 ft 11.5 in (3.64 m)	

In 1938, the Soviet collective headed by Andrei N Tupolev designed the ANT-58 to meet an official specification for a sturdy twin-engined bomber able to carry a crew of three plus a 4,410 lb (2,000 kg) bomb load, and capable of level and diving attacks. An attractive mid-wing monoplane with twin fins and rudders, the ANT-58 first flew on 29 January 1941. Despite problems with its 1,400 hp AM-37 engines, the bomber had an exceptional performance, and development proceeded through two further prototypes, the four-seater ANT-59 and ANT-60, the latter having M-82 (later ASh-82) radials.

In 1942 work was started on a pre-production series of aircraft under the official designation Tu-2, and three of these first saw action later that year. The new bomber, which had excellent handling characteristics, was received enthusiastically, and after extensive structural modification to simplify construction it went into full production as the Tu-2S, with 1,850 hp M-82FN engines. Quantity deliveries began early in 1944. By the end of the war in Europe, 1,111 had been built.

Development continued during and after the war, with various engine and armament installations being tested. Photographic reconnaissance, torpedo-bomber and ground-attack variants were also produced.

Production of the basic Tu-2 continued until 1947, when 3,000 had been delivered to the Soviet Air Force, China, Poland, and other Communist countries. Later aircraft were

MUZEUM WOJSKA POLSKIEGO		
OWNER/OPERATOR :		Polish Army
ADDRESS	:	Al Jerozolimskie 3, Warszawa 00-950, Poland
LOCATION	:	In Warsaw city centre near the river Vistula
ADMISSION	:	Daily: Monday, Thursday, Saturday 1200-1700; Wednesday 1300-1900; Friday 1000-1500; Sunday 1030-1700
FURTHER INFO	:	The army museum in fact covers the history of all the Polish armed forces. In addition to a large collection of military vehicles and artillery items, the museum has a number of Russian military aircraft on display.

powered by ASh-82FNV engines driving four-bladed airscrews. A lighter training development, the UTB, was developed by Sukhoi, and a number of these were supplied to the Polish Air Force.

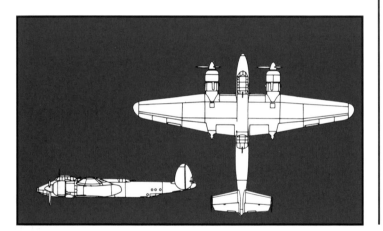

TUPOLEV Tu-2
COUNTRY OF ORIGIN
USSR
ENGINES
two Shvestov M-82 14-cylinder radial air-cooled, 1,850 hp each
CREW
four
MAX SPEED
342 mph (550 km/h) at 17,720 ft (5,400 m)

RANGE
1,243 miles (2,000 km)
CEILING
31,200 ft (9,500 m)
LENGTH
45 ft 3 in (13.80 m)
SPAN
61 ft 10.5 in (18.85 m)
HEIGHT
13 ft 11 in (4.25 m)

A quantum leap forward in terms of speed and comfort for passengers on short- and medium-haul routes occurred with the introduction of gas turbine-powered airliners. The first, by a long way, was the Vickers Viscount which went on to become the most successful airliner ever built.

Following their success with the Viking piston-engined airliner, Vickers embarked on the new project as a result of recommendations from the Brabazon Committee, set up by the British government to advise on the post-war development of the civil aviation industry.

The initial Viscount was the V.630, the world's first propeller-turbine airliner. It made its first flight on 16 July 1948 and was put into service by BEA (now British Airways) on the London-Paris and London-Edinburgh routes on an experimental one-month basis. This began on 29 July 1950, so establishing the first turbine-powered scheduled commercial service.

The definitive 700 Series aircraft were followed by the larger, more powerful 800 Series and, in turn, the 810 Series which were ordered not only by airlines, but also by governments and major companies, as VIP and executive transports. Without competition, airlines queued at Vickers door and as a result, the Viscount became the first British airliner to achieve substantial sales in the United States, initially with Capital Airlines.

More than 60 operators in some 40 countries had purchased Viscounts by the time the last machine came off the production line and was delivered to the Civil Aviation Administration of China on 16 April, 1964. Many Viscounts remain in service throughout the world and will do so for years to come.

However, as a complete contrast to a common situation when preservationists find that every example of a type has been scrapped, Air Canada presented one of their Series 700 Viscounts to the National Aviation Museum at Rockcliffe in 1969. At that time, 340 of the 445 built were still in service with operators around the world.

VICKERS VISCOUNT 700	
COUNTRY OF ORIGIN	UK
ENGINES	four Rolls-Royce Dart 505 propeller-turbines, 1,547 ehp each
CREW	two/three
MAX SPEED	302 mph at 20,000 ft (486 km/h at 6,100 m)
RANGE	1,230 miles (1,980 km)
CEILING	27,500 ft (8,380 m)
LENGTH	81 ft 2 in (24.73 m)
SPAN	93 ft 8.5 in (28.56 m)
HEIGHT	26 ft 9 in (8.15 m)

Above: The Viscount is also exhibited at the Wales Aircraft Museum in Cardiff.

The Corsair ranks as one of the truly great fighters of World War II, and remained in production longer than any other US fighter of that war. In response to a 1938 requirement for a single-seat shipboard fighter, Vought designer Rex Beisel took the most powerful engine available and built the smallest possible airframe around it. To keep the undercarriage short despite the large-diameter propeller, the aircraft was given its distinctive inverted gull wing, with the main legs located at the lowest point.

The XF4U-1 prototype first took to the air on 29 May 1940, powered by a 2,000 hp Pratt & Whitney Double Wasp. It proved to be faster than any US fighter then flying, and was ordered into production, deliveries of the F4U-1 beginning in October 1942. As well as serving with the US Marines and Navy, Corsairs were supplied to Britain's Royal Navy under Lend-Lease, and also to the Royal New Zealand Air Force. Fleet Air Arm Corsairs based in HMS *Victorious* saw action on 3 April 1944, during the attacks on the *Tirpitz*. In the Pacific theatre the Corsair quickly demonstrated its superiority over its Japanese opponents; Marine Corps F4Us destroyed no fewer than 584 enemy aircraft by the end of 1943.

There was a range of developments and variants to suit specific roles, and even the end of the war failed to stop Corsair

production. The XF4U-6, redesignated AU-1, served with the Marines in Korea, and the final variant, the F4U-7, was used by the US Navy and also by the Aéronavale, with whom it served in Indochina. Production ended in December 1952.

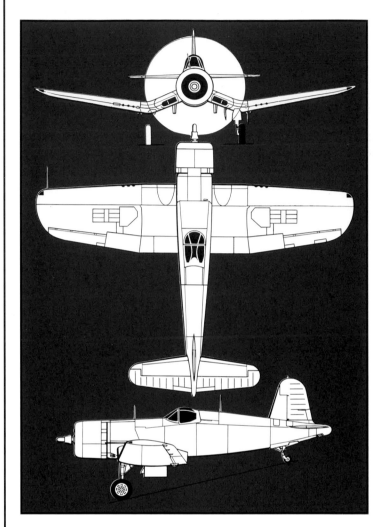

THE AIR MUSEUM – PLANES OF FAME EAST

OWNER/OPERATOR :	Bob Pond	
ADDRESS	:	14771 Pioneer Trail, Eden Prairie, Minnesota 55344
LOCATION	:	Flying Cloud Airport, 12 miles southeast of Minneapolis. Road – County Road 1
ADMISSION	:	May-September 1100-1700 Saturday-Sunday or by appointment
FURTHER INFO	:	In the words of aviation museum specialist Bob Ogden, 'The fine condition of the aircraft and the nature of their surroundings makes this collection one of the most impressive in the USA'.

VOUGHT F4U-1D CORSAIR

COUNTRY OF ORIGIN

USA

ENGINES

Pratt & Whitney R-2800-8W double Wasp 18-cylinder radial air-cooled, 2,000 hp

CREW

one

MAX SPEED

425 mph (684 km/h) at 20,000 ft (6,100 m)

RANGE

1,015 miles (1,635 km)

CEILING

37,000 ft (11,280 m)

LENGTH

33 ft 4.5 in (10.16 m)

SPAN

41 ft (12.47 m)

HEIGHT

15 ft 1 in (4.60 m)

The world's first successful single-main-rotor helicopter, the VS-300 is the progenitor of today's most prolific rotorcraft family. Igor Sikorsky had first experimented with helicopters in Russia in 1910, but it was not until the late 1920s, when he was engineering manager of Vought Sikorsky in the USA, that he returned to the problem. In 1939 he designed and built the VS-300, and on September 14 he made his first tentative flights. The structure was kept simple for ease of modification, and the machine underwent more than 200 alterations, including several complete rebuilds. Over the following two years it became known as 'Igor's Nightmare'.

Originally it featured a basic airframe with the pilot seated in front of the 90 hp Lycoming engine, which drove a single three-bladed main rotor and a tail rotor on a rear boom which also carried a large vertical surface for yaw control.

The boom was then replaced by a longer steel-tube structure which carried three tail rotors, on one horizontal and two vertical shafts, counteracting the torque of the main rotor. This arrangement gave way to a single rotor on a vertical shaft and one working in the horizontal plane, and, finally, to the single anti-torque tail rotor.

Two-minute tethered flights were being made by November 1939, and the ropes were abandoned on 13 May 1940, by which time a 100 hp Franklin engine was fitted. The VS-300 was also equipped with pontoons and flown from water. Flight duration steadily increased until, on 6 May, 1941 Sikorsky set a world helicopter endurance record of 1 hour 32 minutes 26.1 seconds. This historic machine is now a prized exhibit in the Henry Ford Museum at Dearborn, Michigan, USA.

THE HENRY FORD MUSEUM AND GREENFIELD VILLAGE	
OWNER/OPERATOR :	The Edison Institute
ADDRESS :	2090 Oakwood Boulevard, Dearborn, Michigan 48121
LOCATION :	12 miles west of Detroit. Road – off Highway 12
ADMISSION :	Daily 0900-1700
FURTHER INFO :	The aeronautical section includes a number of famous aircraft which have contributed to aviation history. Greenfield village covers 240 acres and includes the Wright Brothers original cycle shop, transported here in 1938.

VOUGHT-SIKORSKY VS-300

COUNTRY OF ORIGIN
USA

ENGINES
one 90 hp Lycoming air-cooled inline

CREW
one

MAX SPEED
n/a

ENDURANCE
1 hour 32 minutes

CEILING
n/a

LENGTH
n/a

ROTOR DIAMETER
28 ft 0 in (8.68 m)

HEIGHT
n/a

In the early 1930s commercial air transport was revolutionized by the appearance in the USA of a new breed of all-metal monocoque single-engined monoplane airliners. One of these was the six-passenger Vultee V1, designed by Gerard Vultee. It first flew on 19 February 1933, powered by a 650 hp Wright Cyclone F2 radial engine. Tests showed that the V1 had an exceptional performance, and the Airplane Development Corporation, its manufacturer, won an order from American Airlines for 20 production V1-As.

By September 1934, the airline had eight in service on the St Louis to Chicago run, which it covered in 99 minutes. On one test flight the airline's chief pilot flew from Chicago to Newark, New Jersey, in just under three hours – 11 minutes faster than the record, which was held by a single-seat racing aircraft. In January 1934 'Jimmy' Doolittle had made a transcontinental flight in the demonstrator V1-A from Burbank, California, to Floyd Bennett Field, New York, in just under 12 hours, but this record was cut by a further 25 minutes some six weeks later by Leland Andrews, in the same aircraft. Andrews later set a record of 8 hours 8 minutes for a 1,620-mile (2,952 km) flight from Los Angeles to Mexico City.

American Airlines took only 13 of its 20 aircraft, but 27 V1-As were built before legislation was passed in October 1934 making it mandatory for all commercial passenger aircraft in the USA to have two or more engines. By this time the V1-A was also being superseded by more advanced types. Subsequently, several V1-As (and the V1) found their way to Spain and were flown by both sides in the Spanish Civil War. Some were also sold to China.

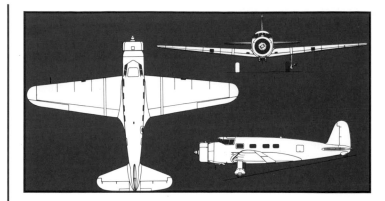

VIRGINIA AVIATION MUSEUM

OWNER/OPERATOR	:	Virginia Aeronautical Society
ADDRESS	:	PO Box 787, Ashland, Virginia 23005
LOCATION	:	Byrd International Airport, 5 miles east of Richmond. Road – off Route 60
ADMISSION	:	Daily 0900-1630
FURTHER INFO	:	The collection, founded by the late Sidney Shannon, includes a number of rare classic aircraft which are mostly in flying condition.

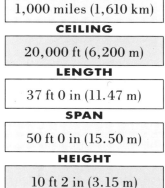

VULTEE V1-A

COUNTRY OF ORIGIN

USA

ENGINES

one 735 hp Wright Cyclone SR-1820-F2 air-cooled radial

CREW

two

MAX SPEED

235 mph (378 km/h)

RANGE

1,000 miles (1,610 km)

CEILING

20,000 ft (6,200 m)

LENGTH

37 ft 0 in (11.47 m)

SPAN

50 ft 0 in (15.50 m)

HEIGHT

10 ft 2 in (3.15 m)

A single-seat carrier-borne strike aircraft, the Wyvern was designed from the outset to be powered by a propeller turbine. However, because such engines did not become available until 1948, the first examples, designated Wyvern T.F.1, had 2,690 hp Rolls-Royce Eagle piston engines. The first prototype Wyvern made its maiden flight on 16 December 1946, and the example which survives today in the Fleet Air Arm Museum, VR137, is one of seven 'production' T.F.1s. These aircraft were soon succeeded by the Wyvern T.F.2, the first turbine-powered variant, which flew in 1949. One of these had a Rolls-Royce Clyde engine, but the remainder were fitted with the Armstrong Siddeley Python. Thirteen of the 20 ordered were delivered, but the remaining seven were converted to S.4 standard.

The Wyvern S.4, which made its maiden flight in May 1951, was the first variant to reach operational status, seven years after the first Wyvern had flown. This delay was attributable to development problems with the aircraft and its new and untried engines, which led to the loss of several aircraft and test pilots. The S.4 entered service with 813 Squadron, Fleet Air Arm, in May 1953, and first went to sea in HMS *Albion*, in 1954. The type equipped four first-line squadrons, the others being Nos 827, 830 and 831, but No 830, in HMS *Eagle*, was the only unit to fly its Wyverns operationally, using them for ground-attack sorties on Dekheila and Port Said during the Anglo-French intervention in Egypt in November 1956. The last Wyverns were withdrawn from service in March 1958, when 813 Squadron was disbanded at Royal Naval Air Station Ford, Sussex.

THE FLEET AIR ARM MUSEUM

OWNER/OPERATOR	:	The Royal Navy
ADDRESS	:	Royal Naval Air Station, Yeovilton, Ilchester, Somerset BA22 8HT
LOCATION	:	2 miles east of Ilchester. Road – B3151
ADMISSION	:	Daily 1000-1730 (or dusk if earlier)
FURTHER INFO	:	One of the important military aircraft collections in the world, the museum is also home to the Concorde exhibition which features the British prototype 002.

WESTLAND WYVERN S.4

COUNTRY OF ORIGIN	**RANGE**
UK	904 miles (1,455 km)
ENGINES	**CEILING**
Armstrong Siddeley Python ASP3 turboprop 4,110 hp	28,000 ft (8,535 m)
CREW	**LENGTH**
one	42 ft 3 in (12.87 m)
MAX SPEED	**SPAN**
383 mph (606 km/h) at sea level	44 ft 0 in (13.41 m)
	HEIGHT
	15 ft 9 in (4.80 m)

riginating with Bristol Aircraft as the Type 192, the Belvedere was designed to meet a Royal Air Force requirement for a helicopter capable of performing a variety of duties connected with Army operations in the field. These included troop and freight transport, supply dropping, casualty evacuation and paratrooping. Powered by two Napier Gazelle free turbines, the Belvedere was the first twin-engined, twin-rotor helicopter to go into service with the RAF. Its fore and aft rotors were linked by a synchronizing shaft which kept them in phase and allowed them both to be driven by either engine. It could carry 18 fully-armed troops, eight to 12 stretcher cases, or 6,000 lb (2,727 kg) of freight, and bulky loads weighing up to 5,250 lb (2,386 kg) could be slung on a strong point beneath the fuselage.

A total of 26 Belvederes was supplied to the RAF; the first of these flew on 5 July 1958. On 15 September 1961, No 66 Squadron became the first operational RAF unit to be equipped with the type, and in January 1962 the squadron provided support for two Army brigade groups in 'Exercise Lifeline'. Subsequently, the Belvederes of 66 Squadron served in the Middle East, and were also active throughout the Brunei campaign of 1962-66, when they operated from Borneo. The Aden-based Belvederes of 26 Squadron, operating from the Royal Navy carrier *Centaur*, lifted commandos into Tanganyika (Tanzania) during the 1963 rebellion, and the unit later provided support for the Army during the Radfan Operations in South Arabia. The only other unit to operate the Belvedere was 72 Squadron. With the disbanding of 66 Squadron at Seletar in March 1969, the Belvedere was retired from service.

THE INTERNATIONAL HELICOPTER MUSEUM

OWNER/OPERATOR	:	The International Helicopter Museum
ADDRESS	:	Locking Moor Road, Weston-super-Mare, Avon BS22 8PP
LOCATION	:	3 miles southeast of Weston-super-Mare seafront. Road – A368/A371
ADMISSION	:	Daily April-October 1000-1800 (or dusk if earlier); November-March 1030-1600 (not Monday, Tuesday or Friday)
FURTHER INFO	:	The museum houses the world's largest helicopter and autogyro collection and is unique in the UK.

Main picture: Another example on display at the Manchester Air and Space Museum. *Inset*: The Belvedere at the International Helicopter Museum.

WESTLAND BELVEDERE

COUNTRY OF ORIGIN
UK

ENGINES
two Napier Gazelle 100 (NG-A2) free turbines each rated at 1,650 s.h.p

CREW
three/ accommodation twelve

MAX SPEED
138 mph (220 km/h)

RANGE
460 miles (736 km)

CEILING
8,500 ft (2,590 m)

LENGTH
54 ft 4 in (16.56 m)

ROTOR DIAMETER
48 ft 0 in (14.63 m)

HEIGHT
17 ft 3 in (5.26 m)

A two-seat intermediate trainer, the Yak-11 began to enter service with the Soviet Military Aviation Forces in 1947. Its wing planform bore a strong resemblance to that of the earlier Yak-3 and Yak-9 piston-engined fighters, but while they had been powered by well-streamlined liquid-cooled engines, the Yak-11's nose was blunt and housed a Shvetsov ASh-21 seven-cylinder air-cooled radial rated at 730 hp for take-off. The aircraft was of all-metal construction with fabric-covered control surfaces, and for gunnery training, a 7.7 mm machine gun was installed over the port side of the engine. The instructor and pupil were seated in tandem under a single canopy.

The West was unaware of the Yak-11's existence until March 1948, when one was accidentally crash-landed in Turkey, but its outstanding performance was revealed in 1950, when it set a number of FAI-homolgated records in its class, including a 500 m closed-circuit speed of 292.85 mph, a 1,000 km closed-circuit speed of 274.76 mph, a 2,000 km closed-circuit speed of 223.69 mph, and a distance recorded in a straight line of 1,236.64 miles.

Thousands of Yak-11s were built in the Soviet Union and under licence in other Communist countries, and it became one of the world's most widely-used trainers, serving with the air arms of 15 nations, including Albania, Austria, Afghanistan, Bulgaria, China, Czechoslovakia, Egypt, Hungary, Poland, Rumania, Syria and the Yemen. Four were presented to the Austrian Air Force by the Soviet government. Several Yak-11s are now flying in the West. The example depicted belongs to an American private owner.

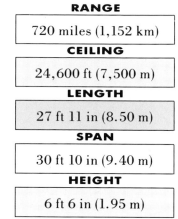

ROBERT F YANCY COLLECTION

OWNER/OPERATOR	:	Robert F Yancy
ADDRESS	:	Klamath Falls, Oregon, USA
ADMISSION	:	Prior permission only
FURTHER INFO	:	The aircraft can be seen at major air races in the United States, especially Reno.

YAKOVLEV Yak-11

COUNTRY OF ORIGIN	
USSR	
ENGINES	
one 730 hp Shvetsov ASh-21	
CREW	
two	
MAX SPEED	
295 mph (472 km/h)	

RANGE	
720 miles (1,152 km)	
CEILING	
24,600 ft (7,500 m)	
LENGTH	
27 ft 11 in (8.50 m)	
SPAN	
30 ft 10 in (9.40 m)	
HEIGHT	
6 ft 6 in (1.95 m)	

The Yak-18 began life as a replacement for the UT-2 primary trainer monoplane, and entered service with the elementary flying training schools of the Soviet Military Aviation Forces in 1946. Originally powered by the 160 hp five-cylinder M-11-FR radial engine in a distinctive helmeted cowling, it was a tandem two-seat monoplane with a semi-retractable main undercarriage and a fixed tailwheel. Although it was simple and rugged, it was light on the controls and stressed for aerobatics, and it soon became popular with pilots. Most Communist air arms used the Yak-18, and it also served with the air forces of Austria and the United Arab Republic.

In 1951 the Yak-18 established several FAI speed records in its class, and four years later the Yak-18U appeared — a version with a tricycle undercarriage and improved engine cowling. However, its overall performance was inferior to that of the original design and it was succeeded by the Yak-18A, introduced in 1957. This had a 260 hp Ivchenko AI-14R nine-cylinder radial fully enclosed by a circular cowling, a larger canopy, greater span and larger vertical tail surfaces. Developed alongside this was the Yak-18P, a fully aerobatic single-seater for competition flying which incorporated several modifications. The Yak-18P entered production in 1961, and at the 1966 Aerobatic Championships at Tushino another development, the Yak-18PM, powered by a 300 hp AI-14RF radial, outflew all of its competitors. Its greatly improved performance included a maximum speed of 196 mph at sea level. Production of the basic Yak-18 trainer terminated at the end of 1967, after 6,760 had been built.

THE EGYPTIAN MILITARY MUSEUM	
OWNER/OPERATOR :	Cairo Museum
ADDRESS :	Cairo, Egypt
LOCATION :	The Egyptian Military Museum is in the citadel in Cairo's city centre
ADMISSION :	Open daily except Friday.

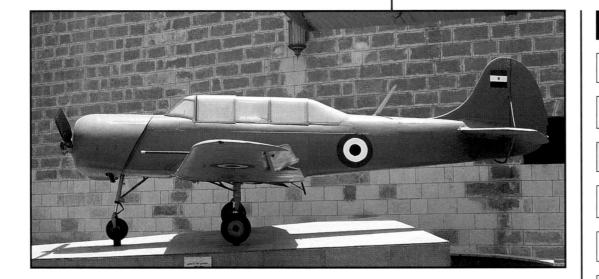

YAKOVLEV Yak-18A	
COUNTRY OF ORIGIN	
USSR	
ENGINES	
Ivchenko A1-14R radial with 9 cylinders air-cooled, 260 hp	
CREW	
two	
MAX SPEED	
163 mph (263 km/h) at sea level	
RANGE	
441 miles (710 km)	
CEILING	
16,600 ft (5,060 m)	
LENGTH	
27 ft 5 in (8.35 m)	
SPAN	
34 ft 9 in (10.60 m)	
HEIGHT	
10 ft 8 in (3.25 m)	

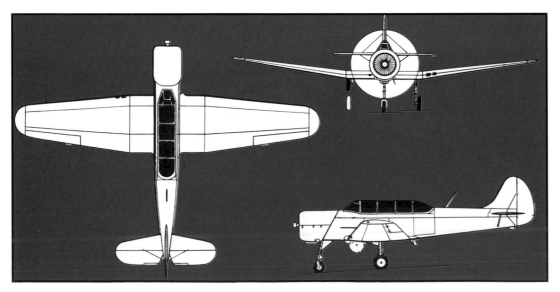

Above: The Yakolev Yak-18 at the Aeronautical Insititute in Peking.
Above left: On display in Cairo.

The Zlin Aviation Company of Czechoslovakia, founded in 1934 and based at Otrokovice, near the town of Zlin, is renowned for its fine trainers and aerobatic aircraft.

In 1947, Zlin won a Czech Ministry of Defence competition for an elementary trainer for use by the Czech Air Force and civilian flying clubs. Orders for the winning design, the Z-26 Trener, eventually totalled 113 aircraft, and it entered Air Force service as the C-5. The aircraft, which had a fabric-covered steel-tube fuselage and wooden wings, had excellent aerobatic qualities, and the Zlin design team developed a range of improved variants. The first was the Z-126 Trener 2, which was all-metal except for its fabric-covered control surfaces and was powered by a 105 hp Walter Minor. Deliveries of the Z-126 began in 1953, and the reputation of Zlin aeroplanes began to spread abroad as aerobatic pilots discovered their potential.

It was the next development, the Z-226, that really established the Zlin reputation. Originally intended as a glider tug, the Z-226 was powered by a 160 hp Walter Minor engine which greatly enhanced the Trener's aerobatic capabilities. This led to the single-seat Z-226A Akrobat, the most successful competition aerobatic aircraft of the late 1950s and early 1960s. Zlin 226 victories included the 1962 world aerobatic competition at Budapest and the Lockheed Trophy at Coventry, in 1957 and in 1963. Zlins also took second and third places. Continual development kept this outstanding family of aeroplanes at the forefront of world aerobatics until the early 1970s.

TECHNICKE MUZEUM V BRNO

OWNER/OPERATOR :		The Brno Technical Museum
ADDRESS	:	Orli 20, 601 86 Brno, Czechoslovakia
LOCATION	:	In the town centre at the junction of Josefka and Orli Streets
ADMISSION	:	Tuesday-Sunday 0900-1700
FURTHER INFO	:	The aviation section of this comprehensive museum majors in instruments and electrical equipment. Most of its collection of aircraft are in store; few are on public view.

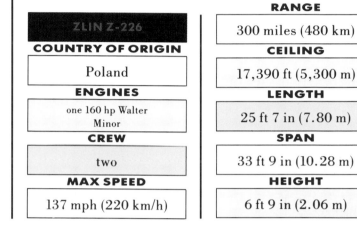

ZLIN Z-226	
COUNTRY OF ORIGIN	**RANGE**
Poland	300 miles (480 km)
ENGINES	**CEILING**
one 160 hp Walter Minor	17,390 ft (5,300 m)
CREW	**LENGTH**
two	25 ft 7 in (7.80 m)
MAX SPEED	**SPAN**
137 mph (220 km/h)	33 ft 9 in (10.28 m)
	HEIGHT
	6 ft 9 in (2.06 m)

UNITED STATES

Aerospace Museum, Hampton, VA
Castle Air Museum, Castle AFB, Atwater, CA
Champlin Fighter Museum, Mesa, AZ
Chanute Air Force Base, Chanute AFB, Rantoul, IL
Combat Jets Flying Museum, Houston, TX
Confederate Air Force (Pacific Wing), Madera, CA
Confederate Air Force, Mesa, AZ
Cradle of Aviation Museum, Garden City, NJ
El Toro Marine Corps Air Station, Santa Ana, CA
Evergreen Air Services, Marana, TX
Experimental Aircraft Association Museum, Oshkosh, WI
Florence Air and Missile Museum, Florence, SC
Grissom Air Force Base Heritage Museum, Grissom AFB, Peru, IN
Henry Ford Museum, Dearborn, MI
Henley Aerodrome and Museum of Transport, Athol, ID
Hurlburt Field Memorial Air Park, Hurlburt Field, FL
Intrepid Sea-Air-Space Museum, USS *Intrepid*, New York, NY
Langley Air Force Base Collection, Hampton, VA
Lone Star Flight Museum, Houston, TX
March Field Museum, Riverside, CA
McClellan Air Force Base, Sacramento, CA
Mud Island, Memphis, TN
Museum of Science and Industry, Chicago, IL
National Air and Space Museum, Silver Hill, MD
National Air and Space Museum, Washington, DC
New England Air Museum, Windsor Locks, CT
Ohio History of Flight, Columbus, OH
Pima Air Museum, Tucso, AZ
Planes of Fame East, Minneapolis, MN
Plattsburgh Military Museum, Plattsburgh AFB, New York, NY
Queen Mary and Spruce Goose, Los Angeles, CA
Robbins Air Force Base Museum of Aviation, Warner Robbins AFB, GA
Selfridge Military Air Museum, Selfridge ANG Base, MI
San Diego Aerospace Museum, San Diego, CA
Strategic Air Command Museum, Offut AFB, Bellville, NE
Travis Air Force Museum, Travis AFB, CA
United States Air Force Museum, Barstow, CA
United States Air Force Museum, Wright Patterson Air Force Base, Dayton, OH
United States Army Transportation Museum, Fort Eustis, VA
Virginia Aviation Museum, Ashland, VA
Wagons to Wings Museum, Morgan Hill, CA
Weeks Air Museum, Tamiami, FL
Wings of Freedom Air and Space Museum, Willow Grove, PA

CANADA

Canadian Museum of Flight, Richmond, BC
Canadian National Exhibition, Toronto ON
Canadian Warplane Heritage, Mount Hope, ON
Kingston City Council, Kingston, ON
National Aviation Museum, Richmond, BC
Royal Canadian Air Force Club, Hamilton, ON
Western Canada Aviation Museum, Winnipeg, MB

UNITED KINGDOM

Aces High, North Weald, Essex
Aerospace Museum, Cosford, Shropshire
AAEE Boscombe Down, Boscombe Down, Wiltshire
Battle of Britain Museum, Hendon, London
Bomber Command Museum, Hendon, London
Fleet Air Arm Museum, Yeovilton, Somerset
Imperial War Museum, Duxford, Cambridgeshire
Imperial War Museum, London
International Helicopter Museum, Weston-super-Mare, Avon
Midland Air Museum, Coventry, West Midlands
The Mosquito Aircraft Museum, London Colney, Herts
Museum of Science and Industry, Manchester
Plane Sailing, Duxford, Cambridgeshire
RAF Museum Collection, RAF Cosford, Shropshire
Royal Museum of Scotland — Museum Flight, East Fortune, Lothian
Science Museum, Yeovilton, Somerset
The Shuttleworth Collection, Hatfield, Herts
The Shuttleworth Collection, Old Warden, Bedfordshire
Ulster Folk and Transport Museum, Holywood, County Down, Northern Ireland
Wales Aircraft Museum, Cardiff

AUSTRALIA

Central Australian Aviation Museum, Alice Springs, NT
Royal Australian Navy Museum, Nowra, NSW
War Memorial, Griffiths, NSW

ALBANIA

War Museum, Gjirokaster

BELGIUM

Musée Royal de L'Armée, Brussels

BRAZIL

Museu de Armas, Bebeduoro
Museu do VARIG, Porto Alegre

CHINA

Aeronautical Institute, Peking
Military Museum, Peking

CUBA

Museo de Playa Giron, Playa Giron

CZECHOSLOVAKIA

Narodni Technicke Muzeum, Prague
Technicke Muzeum v Brne, Brno

DENMARK

Dansk Veteranflysamlung, Stauning

EGYPT

Cairo Museum, Cairo

FINLAND

Keski-Suomen Ilmailumuseo, Tikkakoski

FRANCE

Aero Club de la Somme, Abbeville
Aero Retro, St Rambert d'Albon
L'Amicale Jean-Baptiste Salis, La Ferte Alais
L'Armée de l'Air, Base Aerienne, Reims
Musée Aeronautique de Champagne, Brienne-le-Chateau
Musée d'Avions au Mas Palegry, Perpignan

GERMANY

Auto + Technik Museum, Sinsheim
Deusches Museum von Meisterwerken der Naturwissenschaft und Technik, Munich
Dornier GmbH, Oberpfaffenhofen
Luftfahrtausstellung, Hermeskeil
Luftwaffen Museum, Hamburg
Museum Fur Verhehr Und Technik, Gatow, Berlin
RAF Gutersloh, Gutersloh

INDIA

Indian Air Force Museum, Palam, New Delhi

INDONESIA

Armed Forces Museum, Jakarta

ISRAEL

Israeli Air Force Historical Collection, Beersheba

ITALY

Museo Nazionale dell Scienze e della Tecnica, Milan
Museo Storico dell'Aeronautica Militare Italian, Vigna di Valle

KOREA

Korean War Museum, Seoul, South Korea

MALAYSIA

Muzium Negara, Kuala Lumpur

NETHERLANDS

Aviodome, Shipol
Luchtmacht Museum, Soesterberg

NEW ZEALAND

Museum of Transport and Technology, Western Springs, Auckland

POLAND

Muzeum Lotnictwa I Astronautyki, Krakow
Muzeum Oreza Polskiego, Kolobrzeg
Muzeum Wojska Polskiego, Warsaw

SOUTH AFRICA

South African Air Force Museum, Lanseria
South African Air Force Museum, Snake Valley

SPAIN

Museo del Aire, Madrid

SWEDEN

Svedino's Bil Och Flygmuseum, Ugglarp
Flygvapenmuseum Malmer, Liknopen

SWITZERLAND

Museum der Schweizerischen Fliergertruppe, Dubendorf
Verkehrshaus der Schweiz, Lucerne

THAILAND

Royal Thai Air Force Museum, Bangkok

USSR

Air Force Museum, Monino

VIETNAM

Ba'o Tang Quan Ch'ung Khong-Quancc, Hanoi

Italic page numbers refer to illustrations.

A

Achgelis, Gerd 42
airliners –
    Douglas DC-3 Dakota 6, 35, *35*
    Vickers Viscount 85, *85*
    Vultee V1-A 88, *88*
Albatross D.111 21
Allison J33-A35 engine 61
Alvis Leonides engine 76
Andrews, Leland 88
anti-submarine aircraft –
    Consolidated PBY Catalina 23, *23*
    Fairey Firefly AS.6 40
    Grumman S2 Tracker 49, *49*
    Short S.25 Sunderland 77, *77*
    Sikorsky S-58 79, *79*
Apollo 15z 7
Arab-Israeli War 25
Arado Ar.196z 10, *10*
Argentina –
    Fabrica Militar de Aviones (FMA) 1A-58 Pucara 41, *41*
Argus As8 engine 42
Armstrong Siddeley –
    Lynx engine 11
    Python engine 89
Australia –
    de Havilland D.H.A.3 Drover 32, *32*
Austria –
    Knoller C.II 58, *58*
Austro-Daimer engine 58
Avro –
    504 11
    643 Cadet 11, *11*
    683 Lancaster 7, 12, *12*
    698 Vulcan 13, *13*
    Canada Arrow Interceptor 16
    Canada CF-100 Canuck 14, *14*
    Manchester 12
    Orenda engine 14
    Tutor 11

B

B-34A Lexington 59
B-34B trainer aircraft 59
BAC TSR-2 7
Barnwell, Capt Frank S 21
Bay of Pigs landing 53
Beamont, Roland 38
Bedford, Bill 54
Beisel, Rex 86
Berlin Airlift 50, 77
Bornardi, Major Mario do 62
Biafra War 56
BMW –
    132K engine 10
    323R-2 engine 33
    801C-1 engine 43
Boeing –
    2707-300 15
    B-17 Fortress 6, 17, *17*
    B-29 Superfortress 18, *18*
    B-45 Tornado 20
    B-47 Stratojet 20, *20*
    C-97 Stratofreighter 19, *19*
bombers –
    Avro 683 Lancaster 7, 12, *12*
    Avro 698 Vulcan 13, *13*
    Avro Manchester 12
    B-34A Lexington 59
    B-45 Tornado 20
    Boeing B-17 Fortress 17, *17*
    Boeing B-29 Superfortress 18, *18*
    Boeing B-47 Stratojet 20, *20*
    Convair B-36 24, *24*
    de Havilland D.H.98 Mosquito 30, *30*
    Douglas B-18 Bolo 34, *34*
    Fairey Firefly 40, *40*
    Focke-Wulf Fw 190 43, *43*
    Grand Slam bomb 12
    Grumman TBF Avenger 48, *48*
    Hawker Hurricane 7, 51, *51*
    Ilyushin IL-28 56, *56*
    Junkers Ju 87 Stuka 57, *57*
    Knoller C.II 58, *58*
    Lockheed F-80 Shooting Star 60, *60*
    Lockheed PV-1 Ventura 59, *59*
    McDonnel F2H Banshee 63, *63*
    Messerschmitt Me 262 64, *64*
    Mosquito 7

C

Camm, Sir Sydney 52
Campbell Black, Tom 28
Canada –
    Avro 683 Lancaster 12
    Avro Canada CF-100 Canuck 14, *14*
Caquot, General 6
Catalina 23, *23*
Cathcart-Jones, Owen 28
Chadwick, Roy 12
Chanute, Octave 24
China –
    Z-5 66
Cobham, Sir Alan, "Flying Circus" 11
COIN aircraft 45
Comet Racer 28, *28*
Concorde 15, *15*
Consolidated PBY Catalina 23, *23*
Continental R-670-5 engine 80
Convair B-36 24, *24*

D

Dam Busters 12
Dassault MD.450 Ouragan 25, *25*
de Havilland –
    (Australia) D.H.A.3 Drover 32, *32*
    CS2F-1 49
    D.H.100 Vampire 31, *31*
    D.H.82 Tiger Moth 26, *26*
    D.H.87B Hornet Moth 27, *27*
    D.H.88 Comet Racer 28, *28*
    D.H.90 Dragonfly 29, *29*
    D.H.98 Mosquito 30, *30*
    Goblin engine 31
    Gypsy Major engine 26, 27, 29, 32, 75
    Gypsy Moth 27
    Gypsy Six R engine 28
de Havilland, Geoffrey 28, 29, 30
Denmark –
    Sai KZ II Kupe 75, *75*
Donaldson, Gp Capt E M 46
Doolittle, Major James 69, 88
Dornier Do.24 33, *33*
Douglas –
    B-18 Bolo 34, *34*
    Boeing B-47 Stratojet 20
    C-118 37
    C-124 Globemaster II 36, *36*
    DC-3 Dakota 6, 35, *35*
    DC-6 37, *37*
    R6D Liftmaster 37
    RC-188 37
Duke, Neville 52

E

Egypt, Anglo-French intervention 89
English Electric Lightning 38, *38*
Enola Gay 18, *18*

F

Fabrica Militar de Aviones (FMA) 1A-58 Pucara 41, *41*
Fairchild –
    C-119 Flying Boxcar 39, *39*
    C-82A Packet 39
Fairey Firefly 40, *40*
Falklands War 13, 41, 54
Fiat AS6 engine 62
fighters –
    Avro Canada CF-100 Canuck 14, *14*
    Bristol F.2B 21, *21*
    Dassault MD.450 Ouragan 25, *25*
    de Havilland D.H.100 Vampire 31, *31*
    English Electric Lightning 38, *38*
    Fabrica Militar de Aviones (FMA) 1A-58 Pucara 41, *41*
    Focke-Wulf Fw 190 43, *43*
    Gloster Meteor 46, *46*
    Hawker Hunter 52, *52*
    Hawker Hurricane 51, *51*
    Hawker P.1127 Kestrel 54, *54*
    Hawker Sea Fury 53, *53*
    Lockheed F-80 Shooting Star 60, *60*
    McDonnell F2H Banshee 63, *63*
    Messerschmitt Me 262 64, *64*
    Mikoyan-Gurevich MiG-15 65, *65*
    North American F-86 Sabre 71, *71*
    North American P-51 Mustang 70, *70*
    PZL P-11 73, *73*
    Republic P-47 Thunderbolt 74, *74*
    Sud-Ouest S.O.4050 Vautour 81, *81*
    Supermarine Spitfire 7, 82, *82*
    Vought F4U Corsair 86, *86*
floatplane 67, *67*
flying-boats 23, *23*, 77, *77*
Focke-Wulf –
    Fw44 Stieglitz 42, *42*
    Fw 190 43, *43*
Fokker F.VII/3m 44
Ford 4-AT Tri-Motor 44, *44*
Fouga –
    C.M. 170 Magister 45, *45*
    C.M. 175 Zephyr 45
France –
    British Aircraft Corporation/Aerospatiale Concorde 15, *15*
    Dassault MD.450 Ouragan 25, *25*
    Fouga C.M. 170 Magister 45, *45*
    Fouga C.M. 175 Zephyr 45
    Sud-Ouest S.O.4050 Vautour 81, *81*

G

General Electric –
    J33-A-23 engine 60
    J47 engine 24
    J47-GE-17B engine 71
    J47-GE-25 engine 20
    YN93-GE-3 engine 72
Germany –
    Arado Ar. 196 10
    Bucker Bu131 Jungmann 22, *22*
    Bucker Bu133 Jungmeister 22, *22*
    Dornier Do.24 33, *33*
    Focke-Wulf Fw44 Stieglitz 42, *42*
    Focke-Wulf Fw2 190 43, *43*
    Junkers Ju 87 Stuka 57, *57*
    Messerschmitt Me 262 64, *64*
Gloster –
    Meteor 46, *46*
    Reaper 46, *46*
Gnome-Rhone 14 N7 engine 73
Grand Slam bomb 12
Grumman –
    C-1A Trader 49, *49*
    E-1B Tracer 49
    J2F Duck 47, *47*
    S2 Tracker 49, *49*
    TBF Avenger 48, *48*

H

Handley Page –
    Hastings 50, *50*
    Victor 13
Hawker –
    Fury 53
    Harrier 54
    Hunter 52, *52*
    Hurricane 7, 51, *51*
    P.1127 Kestrel 54, *54*
    Sea Fury 53, *53*
helicopters –
    MIL Mi-4 66, *66*
    Sikorsky S-58 79, *79*
    Vought-Sikorsky VS-300 87, *87*
    Westland Belvedere 90, *90*
Hirth HW 504 engine 22

Hispano-Suiza Nene engine 25
Hitachi HA-13 engine 83
Hofschneider, Kurt 26
Hornet Moth 27, *27*
Hughes H.4 Hercules 55, *55*
Hughes, Howard 55

I

Ilyushin IL-28 56, *56*
interceptors 16, 43, 60
Italy –
    Macchi M.39 62, *62*
Ivchenko Ai-14R engine 92

J

Japan –
    Tachikawa Ki-36 83, *83*
Junkers –
    Ju 52/3m 44
    Jumo engine 43, 57, 64

K

Kartveli, Alexander 74
Kawanishi NI KI 10, *10*
Klimov VK-1 engine 56
Knoller C.II 58, *58*
Knoller, Professor Richard 58
Korean War 36, 39, 40, 53, 56, 60, 63, 65, 71, 77, 86

L

Langley, Samuel P 6
Lindbergh, Charles –
    Spirit of St Louis 18
Lockheed –
    Boeing B-47 Stratojet 20
    F-80 Shooting Star 60, *60*
    T2-V 61
    T-33 Shooting Star 61, *61*
Lycoming engines 32, 87

M

McDonnell F2H Banshee 63, *63*
MacRobertson England to Australia air race 28
Maxim, Sir Hiram 6
Memphis Belle 17, *17*
Messerschmitt Me 262 10, 64, *64*
Midway, Battle of 48
Mikoyan-Gurevich MiG-15 65, *65*
MIL Mi-4 66, *66*
Mil, Mikhail L 66
Mollison, Jim and Amy 28
Mosquito 7, 30, *30*
Mystère IV 25

N

Napier Gazelle engine 90
Noorduyn Norseman 67, *67*
Noorduyn, R B C 67
North American –
    AT-6 Texan/Harvard 68, *68*
    B-25 Mitchell 69, *69*
    F-86 Sabre 71, *71*
    XB-70 Valkyrie 7, 72, *72*
nuclear weapons 13, 18

P

Packard Merlin engine 70
Parot, Jean Charles 81
Poland –
    PZL P-11 73, *73*
    Zlin Z-226 93, *93*
Pratt & Whitney –
    R2800-52W engine 37
    R4360-75 engine 19
    Rwin Pac engine 66
    Wasp engine 23, 24, 36, 44, 47, 55, 59, 68, 74, 86
Pulawski, Zygmunt 73
PZL P-11 73, *73*

R

racing aircraft –
    de Havilland D.H.88 Comet Racer 28, *28*
    Macchi M.39 62, *62*
Radfan Operations 90
reconnaissance aircraft –
    Arado Ar.196 10, *10*
    Douglas C-118 37
    Fairchild C-119 Flying Boxcar 39
    Knoller C.II 58, *58*
    RB-36F and RB-36H 24
    Sud-Ouest S.O.4050 Vautour 81, *81*
    Tachikawa Ki-36 83, *83*
    Tupolev Tu-2 84, *84*

North American B-25 Mitchell 69, *69*
North American XB-70 Valkyrie 72, *72*
Sud-Ouest S.O.4050 Vautour 81, *81*
Tachikawa Ki-36 83, *83*
Tupolev Tu-2 84, *84*
"V" 13
Westland Wyvern 89, *89*
Bristol –
    Centaurus engine 53
    F.2B Fighter 21, *21*
    Hercules engine 50
    Jupiter engine 73
    Mercury engine 73
    Pegasus engine 77, 78
Bristol Siddeley –
    Olympus engine 13, 16
    Pegasus engine 54
Britain, Battle of 57
British Aircraft Corporation –
    English Electric Lightning 38, *38*
    TSR.2 16, *16*
British Aircraft Corporation/Aerospatiale Concorde 15, *15*
British North Greenland Expedition (1951-54) 77
Brunei campaign 90
Bucker –
    Bu131 Jungmann 22, *22*
    Bu133 Jungmeister 22, *22*
Byrd, Lt Cdr Richard 44

replica aircraft 7
Republic P-47 Thunderbolt 74, *74*
Rolls-Royce –
    Avon engine 52
    Avro 683 Lancaster 12, *12*
    Dart engine 70, 85
    Derwent engine 46
    Eagle engine 89
    Falcon engine 21
    Griffon engine 40
    Merlin engine 12, 30, 51, 82
    Nene engine 25, 65
    RB.108 engine 78
    Snecma Olympus engine 15
    Vulture engine 12
Rumpler Taube 7
Ryokichi Endo 83

S
Sai KZ II Kupe 75, *75*
Schneider Trophy Races 62
Scott, C W A 28
Scottish Aviation Twin Pioneer 76, *76*
seaplanes –
    Arado Ar196 10, *10*
    Consolidated PBY Catalina 23, *23*
    Dornier Do.24 33, *33*
    Fouga C.M. 175 Zephyr 45
    Hawker Sea Fury 53, *53*
    Lockheed T2-V 61
    McDonnell F2H Banshee 63, *63*
    Sea Harrier 54
    Sea Hurricane (Hurricat) 51
    Supermarine S-6B seaplane 82
Selfridge, Lt Thomas 71
Short –
    S.25 Sunderland 77, *77*
    S.C.1 78, *78*
Shvetsov –
    ASh-21 engine 91
    ASh-82FNV engine 84
    ASh-82V engine 66
    M-82 engine 84
Siemens SH14a engine 42
Sikorsky S-58 79, *79*
Sikorsky, Igor 87
Sino-Japanese War 83
Spain –
    Bucker Bu131 and Bu133 22
Spanish Civil War 88
Stearman Model A75 Kaydet 80, *80*
Stone, E F 47
Sud-Ouest S.O.4050 Vautour 81, *81*
Suez crisis 56
Supermarine –
    S-6B seaplane 82
    Spitfire *7*, 82, *82*
supersonic aircraft –
    Boeing 2707-300 15
    Concorde 15, *15*
    English Electric Lightning 38, *38*
    Tupolev TU-144 15
Sweeney, Lt Col Charles W 18
Switzerland –
    Bucker Bu131 and Bu133 22

T
Tank, Kurt 42, 43
Tarpon 48
Tibbets, Col Paul W 18
Tiger Moth 26, *26*
Toofani 25, *25*
trainer aircraft –
    Avro Cadet 11, *11*
    Avro Tutor 11
    B-34B 59
    Bucker Bu131 Jungmann 22, *22*
    Bucker Bu133 Jungmeister 22, *22*
    de Havilland D.H.82 Tiger Moth 26, *26*
    de Havilland D.H.87B Hornet Moth 27, *27*
    Focke-Wulf Fw44 Stieglitz 42, *42*
    Fouga C.M. 170 Magister 45, *45*
    Lockheed T-33 Shooting Star 61, *61*
    Mikoyan-Gurevich MiG-15UTI 65
    North American AT-6 Texan/Harvard 68, *68*
    Stearman Model A75 Kaydet 80, *80*
    Tupolev UTB 84
    Yakovlev Yak-11 91, *91*
    Yakovlev Yak-18 92, *92*
    Zlin Z-226 93, *93*
transporters –
    Boeing C-97 Stratofreighter 19, *19*
    de Havilland D.H.A. 3 Drover 32, *32*

Douglas C-118 37, *37*
Douglas C-124 Globemaster II 36, *36*
Douglas R6D Liftmaster 37
Fairchild C-119 Flying Boxcar 39, *39*
Fairchild C-82A Packet 39
Ford 4-AT Tri-Motor 44, *44*
Grumman J2F Duck 47, *47*
Handley Page Hastings 50, *50*
Hughes H.4 Hercules 55, *55*
MIL Mi-4 66, *66*
Scottish Aviation Twin Pioneer 76, *76*
Sikorsky S-58 79, *79*
Westland Belvedere 90, *90*
Trent, L R 59
Tupolev TU-144 15
Tupolev, Andrei N 84
Turbomeca –
    Astazou XV1G engine 41
    Marbore II engine 45

U
Udet, Ernst 42
Union of Soviet Socialist Republics –
    Ilyushin IL-28 56, *56*
    Mikoyan-Gurevich MiG-15 65, *65*
    MIL Mi-4 66, *66*
    Tupolev TU-144 15
    Tupolev Tu-2 56, *56*, 84, *84*
    Yakovlev Yak-11 91, *91*
    Yakovlev Yak-18 92, *92*
United Kingdom –
    Avro 643 Cadet 11, *11*
    Avro 683 Lancaster 12, *12*
    Avro 698 Vulcan 13, *13*
    Bristol F.2B Fighter 21, *21*
    British Aircraft Corporation TSR.2 16, *16*
    British Aircraft Corporation/Aerospatiale Concorde
        15, *15*
    de Havilland D.H.100 Vampire 31, *31*
    de Havilland D.H.82 Tiger Moth 26, *26*
    de Havilland D.H.87B Hornet Moth 27, *27*
    de Havilland D.H.90 Dragonfly 29, *29*
    de Havilland D.H.98 Mosquito 30, *30*
    English Electric Lightning 38, *38*
    Fairey Firefly 40, *40*
    Gloster Meteor 46, *46*
    Gloster Reaper 46, *46*
    Handley Page Hastings 50, *50*
    Hawker Fury 53
    Hawker Harrier 54
    Hawker Hunter 52, *52*
    Hawker Hurricane 51, *51*
    Hawker P.1127 Kestrel 54, *54*
    Hawker Sea Fury 53, *53*
    Scottish Aviation Twin Pioneer 76, *76*
    Short S.25 Sunderland 77, *77*
    Short S.C.1 78, *78*
    Supermarine S-6B seaplane 82
    Supermarine Spitfire *7*, 82, *82*
    Vickers Viscount 85, *85*
    Westland Belvedere 90, *90*
    Westland Wyvern 89, *89*
United States of America –
    Boeing 2707-300 15
    Boeing B-17 Fortress 17, *17*
    Boeing B-29 Superfortress 18, *18*
    Boeing B-47 Stratojet 20, *20*
    Boeing C-97 Stratofreighter 19, *19*
    Consolidated PBY Catalina 23, *23*
    Convair B-36 24, *24*
    Douglas B-18 Bolo 34, *34*
    Douglas C-118 37, *37*
    Douglas C-124 Globemaster II 36, *36*
    Douglas DC-3 Dakota 35, *35*
    Douglas R6D Liftmaster 37
    Douglas RC-188 37
    Fairchild C-119 Flying Boxcar 39, *39*
    Fairchild C-82A Packet 39
    Ford 4-AT Tri-Motor 44, *44*
    Grumman C-1A Trader 49, *49*
    Grumman E-1B Tracer 49
    Grumman J2F Duck 47, *47*
    Grumman S2 Tracker 49, *49*
    Grumman TBF Avenger 48, *48*
    Hughes H.4 Hercules 55, *55*
    Lockheed F-80 Shooting Star 60, *60*
    Lockheed PV-1 Ventura 59, *59*
    Lockheed T2-V 61
    Lockheed T-33 Shooting Star 61, *61*
    McDonnell F2H Banshee 63, *63*
    Noorduyn Norseman 67, *67*
    North American AT-6 Texan/Harvard 68, *68*
    North American B-25 Mitchell 69, *69*

North American F-86 Sabre 71, *71*
North American P-51 Mustang 70, *70*
North American XB-70 Valkyrie 72, *72*
Republic P-47 Thunderbolt 74, *74*
Sikorsky S-58 79, *79*
Stearman Model A75 Kaydet 80, *80*
Vought F4U Corsair 86, *86*
Vought-Sikorsky VS-300 87, *87*
Vultee V1-A 88, *88*

V
"V" bombers 13
Vickers –
    Valiant 13
    Viscount 85, *85*
Vinizki, Yuri 66
Vought F4U Corsair 86, *86*
Vought-Sikorsky VS-300 87, *87*
VTOL (Vertical Take-Off and Landing) aircraft 54, *54*
Vultee, Gerard 88
Vultee V1-A 88, *88*

W
Waller, Ken 28
Wallis, Barnes 12
Walter Minor engine 93
Westinghouse J34-WE-38 engine 63
Westland –
    Belvedere 90, *90*
    Wyvern 89, *89*
World War I 21, 58
World War II –
    Arado Ar.196 12
    Boeing B-17 Fortress 17
    Bucker Bu131 Jungmann 22
    Consolidated PBY Catalina 23
    de Havilland D.H.82 Tiger Moth 26
    de Havilland D.H.98 Mosquito 30
    de Havilland trainer aircraft 26, 27

Dornier Do.24 33
Douglas B-18 Bolo 34
Fairey Firefly 40
Focke-Wulf Fw 190 43
Gloster Meteor 46
Grumman TBF Avenger 48
Grumman J2F Duck 47
Hawker Hurricane 51
Hawker Sea Fury 53
Junkers Ju 87 Stuka 57
Lancaster bomber 12
Lockheed F-80 Shooting Star 60
Messerschmitt Me 262 64
North American At-6 Texan/Harvard 68
North American B-25 Mitchell 69
North American P-51 Mustang 70
PZL P-11 73
Republic P-47 Thunderbolt 74
Short S.25 Sunderland 77
Stearman Model A75 Kaydet 80
Supermarine Spitfire 82
Tachikawa Ki-36 83
Vought F4U Corsair 86
Wright –
    Cyclone engine 17, 18, 34, 35, 39, 47, 48, 49, 69,
        88
    J6 Whirlwind engine 44
    R-1820-84 engine 79
Wright Flyer 6, 7

Y
Yakovlev –
    Yak-11 91, *91*
    Yak-18 92, *92*

Z
Z-5 66
Zlin Z-226 93, *93*

ACKNOWLEDGEMENTS

The author and publishers would like to thank the following for providing
photographs:

Peter R Arnold: pp74b, 82t. **Alan Curry:** pp6t, 10, 18b, 25b, 51b, 52
inset, 54, 66b, 88t. **John Downey:** pp6b, 13b, 16b, 89, 90b. **Alan
Green:** pp27t, 70t. **Bob Jackson:** p31t. **Philip Jarrett:** p40.
George Jenks: pp48tr, 50t, 52b, 59, 68tr, 77t. **Mark Harrison:** 41t.
Gerry Manning: pp7t, 8, 9, 12b, 14b, 15t, 16t, 17b, 18t, 20, 21, 22, 23t,
24, 25 inset, 26, 27b, 30, 31b, 34, 35, 36t, 37, 38, 39, 41b, 42t, 43, 44b,
45, 46t, 47, 48b, 49, 51t, 53, 55, 57b, 60b, 61b, 63, 64, 65, 67b, 68tl, 68b,
69t, 70b, 71, 72, 74t, 76b, 77b, 79, 81, 82b, 83, 85b, 87, 88b, 90t, 91, 92.
Bob Ogden: pp17t, 58, 60t, 61t, 62, 66t, 67t, 69c, 73, 75, 76t, 80, 84,
86, 93. **Ian Oliver:** p32. **Lloyd Robinson:** pp11, 78, 85t. **Chris
Walkden:** pp19, 42b, 47 inset, 57 inset.
l = left, r = right, t = top, b = bottom
Illustrations: © Greenborough Associates/Pilot Press
The publishers would also like to thank Bill Broadfoot, Robert Jackson, and
Philip Jarret.